W9-BZD-174

Cisco Networking Academy Program
CCNA 1 and 2 Engineering Journal and Workbook
Revised Third Edition

Cisco Systems, Inc.

Cisco Networking Academy Program

Cisco Press

800 East 96th Street
Indianapolis, IN 46240 USA

Cisco Networking Academy Program
CCNA 1 and 2 Engineering Journal and Workbook
Revised Third Edition

Cisco Systems, Inc.

Cisco Networking Academy Program

Copyright © 2005 Cisco Systems, Inc.

Published by:
Cisco Press
800 East 96th Street
Indianapolis, IN 46240 USA

Printed in the United States of America   1 2 3 4 5 6 7 8 9 0

First Printing August 2004

ISBN: 1-58713-151-X

Trademark Acknowledgments

Warning and Disclaimer

CISCO SYSTEMS

For information on the Cisco Networking Academy Program or to locate a Networking Academy, please visit www.cisco.com/edu.

Corporate and Government Sales

Cisco Press offers excellent discounts on this book when ordered in quantity for bulk purchases or special sales. For more information, please contact: **U.S. Corporate and Government Sales** 1-800-328-3419 corpsales@pearsontechgroup.com

For sales outside of the U.S., please contact: **International Sales** international@pearsontechgroup.com.

Feedback Information

At Cisco Press, our goal is to create in-depth technical books of the highest quality and value. Each book is crafted with care and precision, undergoing rigorous development that involves the unique expertise of members from the professional technical community.

Readers' feedback is a natural continuation of this process. If you have comments regarding how we could improve the quality of this book or otherwise alter it to better suit your needs, you can contact us at networkingacademy@ciscopress.com. Please make sure to include the book title and ISBN in your message.

We greatly appreciate your assistance.

Publisher	**John Wait**
Editor-In-Chief	**John Kane**
Executive Editor	**Mary Beth Ray**
Cisco Systems Representative	**Anthony Wolfenden**
Cisco Press Program Manager	**Nannette M. Noble**
Production Manager	**Patrick Kanouse**
Technical Editor	**Andrew Large**
Compositor	**Mark Shirar**
Cover and Interior Designer	**Louisa Adair**

CISCO SYSTEMS

Corporate Headquarters
Cisco Systems, Inc.
170 West Tasman Drive
San Jose, CA 95134-1706
USA
www.cisco.com
Tel: 408 526-4000
      800 553-NETS (6387)
Fax: 408 526-4100

European Headquarters
Cisco Systems International BV
Haarlerbergpark
Haarlerbergweg 13-19
1101 CH Amsterdam
The Netherlands
www-europe.cisco.com
Tel: 31 0 20 357 1000
Fax: 31 0 20 357 1100

Americas Headquarters
Cisco Systems, Inc.
170 West Tasman Drive
San Jose, CA 95134-1706
USA
www.cisco.com
Tel: 408 526-7660
Fax: 408 527-0883

Asia Pacific Headquarters
Cisco Systems, Inc.
Capital Tower
168 Robinson Road
#22-01 to #29-01
Singapore 068912
www.cisco.com
Tel: +65 6317 7777
Fax: +65 6317 7799

Cisco Systems has more than 200 offices in the following countries and regions. Addresses, phone numbers, and fax numbers are listed on the
Cisco.com Web site at www.cisco.com/go/offices.

Argentina • Australia • Austria • Belgium • Brazil • Bulgaria • Canada • Chile • China PRC • Colombia • Costa Rica • Croatia • Czech Republic
Denmark • Dubai, UAE • Finland • France • Germany • Greece • Hong Kong SAR • Hungary • India • Indonesia • Ireland • Israel • Italy
Japan • Korea • Luxembourg • Malaysia • Mexico • The Netherlands • New Zealand • Norway • Peru • Philippines • Poland • Portugal
Puerto Rico • Romania • Russia • Saudi Arabia • Scotland • Singapore • Slovakia • Slovenia • South Africa • Spain • Sweden
Switzerland • Taiwan • Thailand • Turkey • Ukraine • United Kingdom • United States • Venezuela • Vietnam • Zimbabwe

About the Technical Editor for the Revised Third Edition

Andrew Large, CCNP, CCAI, has been creating networks with Cisco routers and switches since 1992. He became a Regional Cisco Networking Academy instructor in 1998. He has BA, M.Ed., and Ed.S. degrees in elementary education from the University of South Alabama. Andrew has worked as a worldwide trainer for Cisco Systems and served as the team lead for the current BCRAN course and coteam lead for the current CCNP 4 course. Currently, he is an instructor at an inner-city high school, C.F. Vigor High School, in Prichard, Alabama.

Table of Contents

Foreword

Throughout the world, the Internet has brought tremendous new opportunities for individuals and their employers. Companies and other organizations are seeing dramatic increases in productivity by investing in robust networking capabilities. Some studies have shown measurable productivity improvements in entire economies. The promise of enhanced efficiency, profitability, and standard of living is real and growing.

Such productivity gains aren't achieved by simply purchasing networking equipment. Skilled professionals are needed to plan, design, install, deploy, configure, operate, maintain, and troubleshoot today's networks. Network managers must assure that they have planned for network security and for continued operation. They need to design for the required performance level in their organization. They must implement new capabilities as the demands of their organization, and its reliance on the network, expands.

To meet the many educational needs of the internetworking community, Cisco Systems established the Cisco Networking Academy Program. The Networking Academy is a comprehensive learning program that provides students with the Internet technology skills essential in a global economy. The Networking Academy integrates face-to-face teaching, web-based content, online assessment, student performance tracking, hands-on labs, instructor training and support, and preparation for industry-standard certifications.

The Networking Academy continually raises the bar on blended learning and educational processes. The Internet-based assessment and instructor support systems are some of the most extensive and validated ever developed, including a 24/7 customer service system for Networking Academy instructors. Through community feedback and electronic assessment, the Networking Academy adapts the curriculum to improve outcomes and student achievement. The Cisco Global Learning Network infrastructure designed for the Networking Academy delivers a rich, interactive, and personalized curriculum to students worldwide. The Internet has the power to change the way people work, live, play, and learn, and the Cisco Networking Academy Program is in the forefront of this transformation.

This Cisco Press title is one of a series of best-selling companion titles for the Cisco Networking Academy Program. Designed by Cisco Worldwide Education and Cisco Press, these books provide integrated support for the online learning content that is made available to Academies all over the world. These Cisco Press books are the only authorized books for the Networking Academy by Cisco Systems, and provide print and CD-ROM materials that ensure the greatest possible learning experience for Networking Academy students.

I hope you are successful as you embark on your learning path with Cisco Systems and the Internet. I also hope that you will choose to continue your learning after you complete the Networking Academy curriculum. In addition to its Cisco Networking Academy Program titles, Cisco Press also publishes an extensive list of networking technology and certification publications that provide a wide range of resources. Cisco Systems has also established a network of professional training companies—the Cisco Learning Partners—who provide a full range of Cisco training courses. They offer training in many formats, including e-learning, self-paced, and instructor-led classes. Their instructors are Cisco certified, and Cisco creates their materials. When you are ready, please visit the Learning & Events area on Cisco.com to learn about all the educational support that Cisco and its partners have to offer.

Thank you for choosing this book and the Cisco Networking Academy Program.

Kevin Warner
Senior Director, Marketing
Worldwide Education
Cisco Systems, Inc.

Introduction

Cisco Networking Academy Program CCNA 1 and CCNA 2 Engineering Journal and Workbook , Revised Third Edition, is a supplement to your classroom and laboratory experience with the Cisco Networking Academy Program.

This book provides you with additional vocabulary exercises and certification exam review questions and answers. Each chapter also includes concept questions and focus questions that test your knowledge of the networking and routing material in different ways. Concept questions range from real-life scenarios to reflective ideas where the answers are not always obvious. Focus questions provide you with an opportunity to demonstrate and strengthen your understanding of the concepts to continue preparing for the CCNA Certification exam or to pursue a career in the IT industry.

Completing this workbook allows you to develop and express a clear understanding of networking basics, routers and routing basics. You will find that your studies are best complemented by a text that describes the theory and foundational concepts introduced in the course. To that end, the *CCNA 1 and 2 Companion Guide,* Revised Third Edition, includes thorough treatments of the topics and the *CCNA 1 and 2 Lab Companion,* Revised Third Edition, provides opportunities for hands-on experience with the components studied in the course.

The Engineering Journal and Workbook includes writing opportunities that help you learn the types of information that would be relevant to keep in an engineering journal. In addition to the writing opportunities offered in this book, we recommend that you keep a separate technical or engineering journal. Typically, a journal is a paper-bound composition book in which pages are not added or subtracted, but dated. The types of journal entries that are most applicable for Networking Academy students include:

- Daily reflections
- Troubleshooting details
- Lab procedures and observations
- Equipment logs
- Hardware and software notes
- Router configurations

Because the journal becomes much more important as you do more network design and installation work, good habits can be developed by starting with a journal on the first day of the CCNA 1 and keeping it current throughout your course and subsequent IT career.

PART I

CCNA 1: Networking Basics

Introduction to Networking

It is important to be able to recognize and name the major components of a PC for the following three reasons:

- Computers are important network-building devices.

- Many networking devices are special-purpose computers, with many of the same parts as "normal" PCs.

- For you to view the online curriculum, your own computer must be in working order, which means that you might need to occasionally troubleshoot simple problems in your computer's hardware and software.

Concept Questions

Demonstrate your knowledge of these concepts by answering the questions in the Engineering Journal space provided.

1. The transistor and the integrated circuit made modern computers possible. Explain why.

_____

_____

_____

_____

2. If your computer doesn't power up, what steps might you take to identify and correct the problem?

_____

_____

_____

_____

3. Explain how to do the following:

   A. Select the NIC card.

   _____

   _____

   B. Set the correct IP address.

   _____

   _____

   C. Adjust the display (if necessary).

   _____

   _____

D. Install and set up the browser.

_____

_____

Vocabulary Exercise

Define the following terms as completely as you can. Use the online curriculum or CCNA 1 Chapter 1 of the _Cisco Networking Academy Program CCNA 1 and 2 Companion Guide_, Revised Third Edition, material for help.

ASCII

_____

_____

backplane

_____

_____

backplane components

_____

_____

binary

_____

_____

bits

_____

_____

bus

_____

_____

bytes

_____

_____

capacitor

_____

_____

CD-ROM drive

_____

_____

CPU

_____

_____

expansion slots

_____

_____

floppy disk drive

_____

_____

hard disk drive

_____

_____

Hexadecimal

_____

_____

IRQ

_____

_____

LAN

_____

_____

LEDs

_____

_____

microprocessor

_____

monitor connector

_____

_____

motherboard

_____

_____

mouse port

_____

_____

network

_____

_____

network interface card

_____

_____

parallel port

_____

_____

PC components

_____

_____

PCBs

_____

_____

personal computer subsystems

_____

_____

power supply

_____

_____

protocol

_____

_____

RAM

_____

_____

resistor

_____

_____

ROM

_____

_____

serial port

_____

_____

small, discrete components

_____

_____

solder

_____

_____

sound card

_____

_____

subnetwork

_____

_____

subnetwork mask

_____

_____

throughput

_____

_____

transistor

_____

_____

video card

_____

_____

WANs

_____

_____

web browser

_____

_____

Focus Questions

1. What are the major components of a PC?

_____

_____

2. What is the information flow in an idealized computer?

_____

_____

3. What is the relationship of NICs to PCs?

_____

_____

4. Describe the components of a PC compared to those of a laptop.

_____

_____

5. What is data throughput and how does it relate to digital bandwidth?

_____

_____

6. What factors affect bandwidth and throughput? What units measure the quantity of information?

_____

_____

7. How do binary numbers represent alphanumeric data?

_____

_____

8. How do you convert the hexadecimal number 444 to decimal? (Show your work in the space provided.)

_____

_____

CCNA Exam Review Questions

The following questions help you review for the CCNA exam. Answers appear in Appendix B, "CCNA 1 and 2 Exam Review Questions Answer Key."

1. Which of the following best defines networking?

   A. A set of rules or procedures that are either widely used or officially specified

   B. A connection of computers, printers, and other devices for the purpose of communication

   C. A set of rules that govern how computer workstations exchange information

   D. A device that is connected to a computer to provide auxiliary functions

2. Which of the following is not a base 16 number?

   A. CAB

   B. 089

   C. GA6

   D. 222

3. Which of the following terms is used in computing to refer to physical parts or equipment?

   A. Hardware

   B. Software

   C. Protocol

   D. Network

4. Which of the following terms is used in computing to refer to programs or applications?

   A. Hardware

   B. Software

   C. Peripheral

   D. Network

5. Which of the following terms refers to devices that are connected to a computer to provide auxiliary functions such as printing, added disk space, scanning, or CD-ROM?

   A. Protocol

   B. Software

   C. Peripheral

   D. Network

6. Why are individual PCs not efficient or cost effective for business applications?

   A. Individual PC use requires businesses to duplicate equipment and resources.

   B. It is difficult for businesses to communicate quickly or efficiently by using individual PCs.

   C. It is difficult to provide management for operating individual PCs.

   D. All of the above.

7. What is the number 198 in binary?

   A. 01101011

   B. 11000110

   C. 11001100

   D. 11000010

8. What kind of computer operates independently from other computers?

   A. Mainframe

   B. PC

   C. Mac

   D. Standalone

9. What is the hex number C0D in decimal?

   A. 3632

   B. 3005

   C. 3096

   D. 3085

10. What does the term protocol mean in computing terms?

   A. A tool that allows Macintosh and PC computers to communicate with each other

   B. A universal translator that allows different kinds of computers to share data

   C. A description of a set of rules and conventions that govern how devices on a network exchange information

   D. The language that all the computers on a network must use to communicate with each other

11. Which of the following best defines protocol?

    A. A formal description of a set of rules and conventions

    B. A device that is connected to a computer to provide auxiliary functions

    C. A group of people who are assigned to work as a team

    D. The connection of computers, printers, routers, and switches

12. What is the binary number 11100011 in decimal?

    A. 227

    B. 193

    C. 223

    D. 235

13. Why are protocols important?

    A. By setting rules, protocols allow different types of computers to talk to each other.

    B. By consolidating the industry, protocols save companies money.

    C. By forming electronic islands, protocols bypass the sneaker net.

    D. By using common carriers, protocols manage data efficiently.

14. What must all computers on a network be able to do for the network to operate properly?

    A. Print to a local printer

    B. Connect to a telephone line

    C. Use CD-ROMs

    D. Speak the same language

15. A protocol allows which of the following to be linked into a network?

    A. Only PC terminals and workstations

    B. Only Macintosh computers and peripherals

    C. Only PCs to a mainframe

    D. Any type of computer terminal or workstation

Networking Fundamentals

Data networks developed as a result of business applications that had been written for microcomputers. At the time, microcomputers were not connected as mainframe computer terminals were, so there was no efficient way of sharing data between multiple microcomputers. Businesses needed a solution that would successfully address the following three questions:

- How to avoid duplication of equipment and resources
- How to communicate efficiently
- How to set up and manage a network

Local-area networks (LANs) are high-speed, low-error data networks that cover a relatively small geographic area (up to a few thousand meters). LANs connect workstations, peripherals, terminals, and other devices in a single building or another geographically limited area. LANs provide multiple-connected desktop devices (usually PCs) with access to high-bandwidth media. LANs connect computers and services to a common Layer 1 media.

The OSI reference model is a descriptive network scheme whose standards ensure greater compatibility and interoperability between various types of network technologies. Further, the OSI reference model is a way of illustrating how information travels through networks. It is a conceptual framework specifying the network functions that occur at each layer. The OSI model describes how information or data makes its way from application programs (such as spreadsheets) through a network medium (such as wires) to another application program that is located on another computer on a network.

Concept Questions

Demonstrate your knowledge of network fundamentals by answering the following questions in the space provided.

1. What are the major characteristics of a LAN?

_____

_____

2. What are some common networking devices specifically found in LANs?

_____

_____

3. The OSI reference model is a descriptive network scheme whose standards ensure greater compatibility and interoperability between various types of network technologies. Why is such a standard necessary?

_____

_____

4. The OSI reference model organizes distinct functions of a network into seven numbered layers. Briefly describe what each layer does and give two examples of these functions for each layer.

_____

_____

_____

_____

_____

_____

_____

_____

_____

_____

_____

_____

_____

_____

5. Session layer functions coordinate communication interactions between applications. Give an example of how these communication interactions are coordinated.

_____

_____

6. Layer 6 standards also guide how graphic images are presented. What standards for graphic images do Layer 6 employ?

_____

_____

_____

_____

7. Briefly describe how bridges make forwarding decisions.

_____

_____

Vocabulary Exercise

Define the following terms as completely as you can. Use the online curriculum or CCNA 1 Chapter 2 of the *Cisco Networking Academy Program CCNA 1 and 2 Companion Guide*, Revised Third Edition, material for help.

AUI

bandwidth

bridge

broadcast

broadcast domain

bus topology

collision

collision domain

compression

datagram

de-encapsulation

dialog separation

encapsulation

_____

_____

encryption

_____

_____

extended-star topology

_____

_____

extranet

_____

_____

firewall

_____

_____

flooding

_____

_____

frame

_____

_____

full-mesh topology

_____

_____

hierarchical topology

_____

_____

hub

_____

_____

IEEE 802.3

_____

_____

IEEE 802.5

_____

_____

intranet

_____

_____

LAN

_____

_____

Layer 1: physical

_____

_____

Layer 2: data link

_____

_____

Layer 3: network

_____

_____

Layer 4: transport

_____

_____

Layer 5: session

_____

_____

Layer 6: presentation

_____

_____

Layer 7: application

_____

_____

MAC address

_____

_____

MAN

_____

_____

MAU

_____

_____

media

_____

_____

Media Access Control (MAC)

_____

_____

_____

_____

microsegmentation

_____

_____

packet

_____

_____

partial-mesh topology

_____

_____

peer-to-peer

_____

_____

protocol

_____

_____

RAM

_____

_____

repeaters

_____

_____

ring topology

_____

_____

ROM

_____

_____

router

_____

_____

SAN

_____

_____

segment

_____

_____

session

_____

_____

star topology

_____

_____

switch

_____

_____

TCP/IP

_____

_____

TCP/IP application layer

_____

_____

TCP/IP Internet layer

_____

_____

TCP/IP network layer

_____

_____

Focus Questions

1. Briefly list six reasons why a layered network model is used in internetworking.

_____

_____

_____

_____

_____

_____

_____

_____

_____

_____

2. From memory, list the seven layers of the OSI model and briefly describe their function.

_____

_____

_____

_____

_____

_____

_____

_____

_____

_____

_____

_____

_____

_____

_____

_____

3. What is meant by the term *peer-to-peer communication* ?

_____

_____

4. Briefly describe the process of data encapsulation using the following terms: *data*, *segment*, *packet*, *frame*, and *bits*.

_____

_____

_____

_____

_____

_____

_____

_____

5. Describe the information that is added to the data packet as it is encapsulated in the transport, network, and data link layers.

_____

_____

6. What is the OSI reference model?

_____

_____

7. Will networks that are built following the OSI model be identical? Explain.

_____

_____

8. What process does the OSI model describe?

_____

_____

9. What is the importance of the TCP/IP model?

_____

_____

10. How does the OSI model compare with the TCP/IP model?

_____

_____

11. What are the functions and OSI layer of computers, clients, servers, printers, and relational databases?

_____

_____

_____

_____

12. What is the purpose and OSI layer of network interface cards in a LAN?

_____

_____

13. What are the different symbols used for media in a LAN?

14. What is the symbol and purpose of a repeater?

_____

_____

15. What is the function of a hub?

_____

_____

16. What is the purpose of a bridge?

_____

_____

17. What is the purpose of a switch?

_____

_____

18. What is the purpose of a router?

_____

_____

19. What does the cloud in a network topology suggest?

_____

_____

20. What is the purpose of network segments?

_____

_____

21. What is a linear bus network topology?

_____

_____

22. What is a ring network topology?

_____

_____

23. Are the rings of a dual-ring network topology connected? Why or why not?

_____

_____

24. Where is the node of a star network topology located?

_____

_____

25. Where does each node link in an extended star network topology?

_____

_____

26. Which of the following are Layer 5 protocols?

    A. (NFS) Network File System

    B. (SQL) Structured Query Language

    C. (RPC) Remote Procedure Call

    D. X Window System

    E. (ASP) AppleTalk Session Protocol

    F. DNA (Digital Network Architecture)

    G. SCP (Session Control Protocol)

27. What are the advantages of using a layered model for troubleshooting problems?

_____

_____

28. When in the session layer, what are the responsibilities of both hosts when sending a message?

_____

_____

29. What type of two-way communication is the session layer most involved in?

_____

_____

30. What are the most common ways that bandwidth is measured?

_____

_____

31. What are the features of a network that affect throughput?

_____

_____

32. What are the three functions of the presentation layer?

_____

_____

33. At the receiving station, from which layer does the presentation layer get the data?

_____

_____

34. What is a JPEG?

_____

_____

35 .In the presentation layer, what does the algorithm search for to help shrink the size of a file?

_____

_____

36. Use an analogy to describe bandwidth.

_____

_____

37. Compare analog and digital bandwidth.

_____

_____

_____

_____

_____

_____

38.What are the two most important models of network communication?

_____

_____

CCNA Exam Review Questions

The following questions help you prepare for the CCNA exam. Answers also appear in Appendix B, "CCNA 1 and 2 Exam Review Questions Answer Key."

1. What business problem resulting from the proliferation of standalone computers did networks solve?

    A. Inability to communicate and lack of management

    B. Losses due to lack of business by common carriers

    C. Inefficient use of information technology professionals

    D. Increasing level of electromagnetic interference

2. What did early networks allow?

    A. Common carriers to finally make a profit

    B. Workers to copy files onto floppy disks and then carry the disks to a coworker's PC to print

    C. The duplication of resources to expand

    D. The easy and efficient sharing of files and printers

3. Which of the following is *not* a problem that networking helped solve?

    B. Lack of new hardware and software products

    C. Duplication of equipment and resources

    D. Inability to communicate efficiently

4. Why is it desirable to network?

    A. Don't have to duplicate equipment and resources

    B. Makes it easy to communicate quickly and efficiently using standalone computers

    C. Makes it easy to provide management for operating standalone computers

    D. All of the above

5. Why is networking a variety of networks together difficult?

    A. People try to network different types of computer systems together.

    B. Emerging network technologies use different hardware and software specifications.

    C. Incompatibility results from hardware changes.

    D. Computer designers try to make their own protocols, and they are incompatible.

6. Why are networking standards needed?

    A. Many networks now cover wide geographic areas.

    B. Technologies must be compatible to allow communication.

    C. Hardware and software are continually being redesigned.

    D. LANs, MANs, and WANs use different kinds of equipment.

7. Which one of the following is a TCP/IP model application layer protocol ?

    A. Ethernet

    B. IP

    C. UDP

8. Why did using different hardware and software cause problems after networks were established?

    A. Networks cannot be formed if some people have Macs and others have PCs.

    B. Different hardware and software did not provide auxiliary functions for the users.

    C. Different hardware and software implementations used in the new technologies were incompatible.

    D. Each department or business was unable to act as an electronic island; instead, the departments or businesses were forced to work together.

9. What is a LAN?

    A. A network that connects workstations, terminals, and other devices in a geographically limited area

    B. A network that connects workstations, terminals, and other devices in a metropolitan area

    C. A network that serves users across a broad geographic area and often uses transmission devices that a common carrier provides

    D. A network that covers a larger area than a MAN

10. Which one of the following is a TCP/IP application layer protocol?

  A. HTTP

  B. TCP

  C. FDDI

  D. SNAP

11. What is a network that connects computer equipment in a single building called?

  A. LAN

  B. WAN

  C. MAN

  D. DCN

12. Which of the following best defines *standards*?

  A. A set of rules or procedures that are either widely used or officially specified

  B. A connection of computers, printers, and other devices for purposes of communication

  C. A set of rules that govern how computer workstations exchange information

  D. A device that is connected to a computer to provide auxiliary functions

13. What is the OSI model?

  A. A conceptual framework that specifies how information travels through networks

  B. A model that describes how data makes its way from one application program to another through a network

  C. A conceptual framework that specifies which network functions occur at each layer

  D. All of the above

14. As described by the OSI model, how does data move across a network?

  A. Directly from each layer at one computer to the corresponding layers at another computer

  B. Through wires connecting each layer from computer to computer

  C. Down through the layers at one computer and up through the layers at another

15. Which best defines the function of the lower layers (called the media layers) of the OSI model?

  A. Provide for the accurate delivery of data between computers

  B. Convert data into the 1s and 0s that a computer understands

  C. Receive data from peripheral devices

  D. Control the physical delivery of messages over the network

16. Which of the following describes the host layers of the OSI model?

  A. Control the physical delivery of messages over the network

  B. Make up the lower layers in the OSI model

  C. Contain data that is more like 1s and 0s than like human language

  D. Provide for accurate delivery of data between computers

17. Which of the following is a logical topology?

    A. Token-passing

    B. Bus

    C. Star

    D. Mesh

18. Which layer of the OSI model is concerned with physical addressing, network topology, line discipline, and flow control?

    A. Physical layer

    B. Data link layer

    C. Transport layer

    D. Network layer

19. Which layer of the OSI model provides connectivity and path selection between two end systems where routing occurs?

    A. Physical layer

    B. Data link layer

    C. Network layer

    D. Transport layer

20. Which layer of the OSI model is responsible for reliable network communication between end nodes and provides mechanisms for the establishment, maintenance, and termination of virtual circuits, transport fault detection and recovery, and information flow control?

    A. Physical layer

    B. Data link layer

    C. Network layer

    D. Transport layer

21. Which layer of the OSI model establishes, manages, and terminates sessions between applications and manages data exchange between presentation layer entities?

    A. Transport layer

    B. Session layer

    C. Presentation layer

    D. Application layer

22. Which layer of the OSI model ensures that information sent by the application layer of one system will be readable by the application layer of another system, is concerned with the data structures used by programs, and negotiates data transfer syntax for the application layer?

    A. Transport layer

    B. Session layer

    C. Presentation layer

    D. Application layer

23. Which layer of the OSI model identifies and establishes the availability of intended communication partners, synchronizes cooperating applications, and establishes agreement on procedures for error recovery and control of data integrity?

    A. Transport layer

    B. Session layer

    C. Presentation layer

    D. Application layer

24. Which of the following best defines *encapsulation* ?

    A. Segmenting data so that it flows uninterrupted through the network

    B. Compressing data so that it moves more quickly

    C. Moving data in groups so that it stays together

    D. Wrapping of data in a particular protocol header

25. What type of topology uses a single backbone cable with all nodes connecting directly?

    A. Star

    C. Broadcast

    D. Hierarchical

26. What one of the following is a type of VPN?

    A. internal

    B. access

    C. broadband

    D. external

27. Which layer of the OSI model establishes, manages, and terminates communication between applications?

    A. Application

    B. Presentation

    C. Session

    D. Transport

28. What device is used to connect a LAN to a WAN?

    A. Bridge

    B. Router

    C. Switch

    D. Hub

29. Which of the following is the Layer 3 protocol data unit?

    A. Segments

    B. Packets

    C. Frames

    D. Bits

30. Which of the following is a Layer 4 protocol data unit?

    A. Segments

    B. Packets

    C. Frames

    D. Bits

31. Which best describes the function of the presentation layer?

    A. Establishes, manages, and terminates applications

    B. Supports communication between programs like electronic mail, file transfer, and web browsers

    C. Guides how graphic images, sound, and video are handled

    D. Provides transport services from the host to the destination

32. Which best describes the function of the MAC address on a NIC?

    A. Provides a Layer 2 address

    B. Supports communication between the network layer and the physical layer

    C. Provides a unique flat address assigned my the manufacturer

    D. All of the above

33. Which layer of the OSI model layer handles data encryption?

    A. Application

    B. Presentation

    C. Session

    D. Transport

34. Which of the following is a function of the data link layer?

    A. Adds a destination MAC address to the frame

    B. Supports the network layer

    C. Uses frames as the PDU

    D. All of the above

Networking Media

Electricity is a fact of modern life. We use it to perform a variety of tasks. It is brought to our homes, schools, and offices by power lines that carry it in the form of *alternating current* (AC). Another type of current, called *direct current* (DC), is the current found in a flashlight, car battery, and on the motherboard of a computer.

It is important to understand the difference between these two types of current flow. Direct current flows at a constant value when circuits are turned on. Alternating current rises and falls in current values as power companies manufacture it.

When electricity reaches our homes, schools, and offices, it is carried to appliances and machines via wires concealed in walls, floors, and ceilings. Consequently, inside these buildings, AC power-line noise is all around us. If not properly addressed, power-line noise can present problems for a network.

In fact, as you will discover the more you work with networks, AC line noise coming from a nearby video monitor or hard disk drive can be enough to create errors in a computer system. It does this by burying the desired signals and preventing a computer's logic gates from detecting the leading and trailing edges of the square signal waves. This problem can be further compounded when a computer has a poor ground connection.

The third type of electricity is *static electricity* . This most damaging uncontrollable form of electricity must be dealt with to protect sensitive electronic equipment. Such static discharges can destroy semiconductors and data in a seemingly random fashion as they shoot through a computer like bullets. As it can with problems related to AC line noise, good grounding helps solve problems that arise from electrostatic discharge.

Networking media are the various physical environments through which transmission signals pass. For computers to communicate encoded information with each other, networking media must physically connect them to each other. The networking media used to connect computers varies. Several kinds of network media can be used to connect computers:

- Coaxial cable
- Unshielded twisted-pair (UTP) cable
- Shielded twisted-pair (STP) cable
- Fiber-optic cable

Concept Questions

Demonstrate your knowledge of these concepts by answering the following questions in the space provided.

1. Each wire in a cable can act like an antenna. When this happens, the wire actually absorbs electrical signals from other wires in the cable and from electrical sources outside the cable. If the resulting electrical noise reaches a high enough level, it can become difficult for network interface cards to discriminate the noise from the data signal. When electrical noise on the cable originates from signals on other wires in the cable, this is known as crosstalk. How can you minimize crosstalk?

_____

_____

_____

2. To ensure optimal performance, it is important for the network media to carry the signal from one device to another with as little degradation as possible. In networking, several factors can cause the signal to degrade. Some of these factors are internal, whereas others are external. Name some of the factors that can cause a signal to degrade and how to correct the problem.

_____

_____

_____

_____

3. Inside copper wires, factors such as opposition to the flow of electrons (*resistance*), opposition to changes in voltage (*capacitance*), and opposition to changes in current (*inductance*) can cause signals to degrade. External sources of electrical impulses that can attack the quality of electrical signals on the cable include lighting, electrical motors, and radio systems. These types of interference are referred to as *electromagnetic interference* (EMI) and *radio frequency interference* (RFI). How can you protect your network from RFI?

_____

_____

_____

_____

4. *Networking media* is defined as the various physical environments through which transmission signals pass. Several types of network media can be used to connect computers. Identify these different types of network media.

_____

_____

5. Coaxial cable is a type of network media. Describe how coaxial cable is made.

_____

_____

6. UTP cable is used in a variety of networks. How many wires make up this type of cable?

_____

_____

7. STP cable combines the techniques of shielding, cancellation, and twisting of wires. What is shielding, and why is it important?

_____

_____

8. Fiber-optic cable is a networking medium. How does it carry signals?

_____

_____

9. Various criteria, such as rate of data transfer and expense, help determine which type of media should be used. Which media is the fastest and which is the least expensive?

_____

_____

10. The data link layer of the OSI model provides access to the networking media and physical transmission across the medium. If you were going to build a network, what media would you use and why?

_____

_____

Vocabulary Exercise

Define the following terms as completely as you can. Use the online curriculum or CCNA 1 Chapter 3 from the *Cisco Networking Academy Program CCNA 1 and 2 Companion Guide*, Revised Third Edition, for help.

AC

_____

_____

AM

_____

_____

ampere

_____

_____

analog transmission

_____

_____

angle of incidence

_____

_____

attenuation

_____

_____

backbone

_____

_____

circuits

_____

_____

coaxial cable

_____

_____

collision domain

_____

_____

conductor

_____

_____

crosstalk

_____

_____

DC

_____

_____

digital signal

_____

_____

dispersion

_____

_____

electricity

_____

_____

electrons

_____

_____

EIA

_____

_____

EMI

_____

_____

ESD

_____

_____

fiber-optic cable

_____

_____

FM

_____

_____

IEEE

_____

_____

impedance

_____

_____

latency

_____

_____

media

_____

_____

multimeter

_____

_____

multimode

_____

_____

neutrons

_____

_____

noise

_____

_____

oscilloscope

_____

_____

PM

_____

_____

propagation

_____

_____

protons

_____

_____

reflection

_____

_____

refraction RFI

_____

_____

resistance

_____

_____

router

_____

_____

single-mode

_____

_____

standard

_____

_____

STP switch

_____

_____

Thicknet

_____

_____

Thinnet

_____

_____

TIA

_____

_____

twisted cable

_____

_____

UTP

_____

_____

wavelength

_____

_____

Focus Questions

1. What are some examples of electrical insulators?

_____

_____

2. What are some examples of electrical conductors?

_____

_____

3. What is the formula for calculating electric current?

_____

_____

4. What types of charges repel each other and why?

_____

_____

5. Which direction does DC voltage always flow?

_____

_____

6. When does voltage occur?

_____

_____

7. What is it called when static, or resting, electrons move and a flow of charges is created?

_____

_____

8. What is the difference between AC and DC?

_____

_____

9. How do you measure impedance? What is its abbreviation?

_____

_____

10. What three components are necessary to make up a circuit, and how do they allow the control of current?

_____

_____

11. What equipment do you use to graph electrical waves, pulses, and patterns?

_____

_____

12. What are some of the characteristics of an analog signal?

_____

_____

13. What is an ampere?

_____

_____

14. What are the five sources of noise that can affect a bit on a wire?

_____

_____

15. At what speed do modern networks typically work?

_____

_____

16. Compare and contrast four different Ethernet LAN devices in increasing order of complexity (and typically cost).

_____

_____

17. What are some of the characteristics of STP?

_____

_____

18. What are some of the characteristics of UTP?

_____

_____

19. What are some of the characteristics of coaxial cable?

_____

_____

20. What is the difference between STP and UTP?

_____

_____

21. What are the benefits of using coaxial cable?

_____

_____

22. What are the advantages of fiber-optic cable?

_____

_____

23. What are the disadvantages of fiber-optic cable?

_____

_____

24. What is the medium for wireless communication?

_____

_____

25. What are TIA/EIA standards?

_____

_____

26. How does cancellation reduce signal loss?

_____

_____

27. How many conductors does an RJ-45 jack have?

_____

_____

28. What is a shared media environment?

_____

_____

29. Where on a network do collisions occur?

_____

_____

30. What happens to the signal in a collision?

_____

_____

31. How do you recognize a collision domain?

_____

_____

32. How do repeaters extend collision domains?

_____

_____

33. How do hubs extend collision domains?

_____

_____

34. Do repeaters filter network traffic?

_____

_____

35. What is the four-repeater rule?

_____

_____

36. How can two wireless workstations be networked together without an AP?

_____

_____

37. What is the 802.11b standard?

_____

_____

38. What is the 802.11a standard?

_____

_____

39. What type of connector is used to connect a PC running HyperTerminal to a router console port?

_____

_____

CCNA Exam Review Questions

The following questions help you review for the CCNA exam. Answers appear in Appendix B, "CCNA 1 and 2 Exam Review Questions Answer Key."

1. Which of the following correctly describes the type of signal that the network media carries?

   A. Coaxial cable carries pulses of light.

   B. UTP cable carries impedance signals.

   C. STP cable carries electrical impulses.

   D. Fiber-optic cable carries electrical impulses.

2. Which network media carries pulses of light?

   A. Coaxial cable

   B. Fiber-optic cable

   C. UTP cable

   D. STP cable

3. Which of the following is an external source of degradation of the signal on cabling?

   A. EMI caused by electrical motors

   B. RFI caused by light leakage

   C. Impedance caused by radio systems

   D. RFI caused by lighting

4. Which of the following combinations of charges repel each other?

   A. Positive and positive

   B. Negative and negative

   C. Positive and negative

   D. Neutral and neutral

5. What is the cause of crosstalk?

   A. Cable wires that are too large in diameter

   B. Too much noise in a cable's data signal

   C. Electrical motors and lighting

   D. Electrical signals from other wires in a cable

6. Which one of the following is not a characteristic of 10BASE-T?

  A. Twisted-pair cable

  B. Baseband transmission

  C. T-style connectors

  D. 10 Mbps data rate

7. What is a cost-effective way to limit cable signal degradation?

  A. Specify the maximum cable length between nodes.

  B. Increase the size of the conductors in the cabling.

  C. Improve the type of insulating material.

  D. Use a braid or foil covering on wires as a shield.

8. How can cable signal degradation be limited in a cost-effective way?

  A. Improve the type of insulating material.

  B. Place same-circuit wires close to each other.

  C. Use a braid or foil covering on wires as a shield.

  D. Increase the diameter of the conductor in the cabling.

9. What is cancellation in networking media?

  A. The magnetic fields of same-circuit wires cancel each other.

  B. External magnetic fields cancel the fields inside network cabling.

  C. Wires in the same circuit cancel each other's electrical current flow.

  D. Twisting wire pairs cancels the electrical impedance in the wires.

10. Which of the following describes cancellation in cabling?

  A. Wires in the same circuit cancel each other's electrical current flow.

  B. Twisting wire pairs provides self-shielding within the network media.

  C. The magnetic fields of wires on different electrical circuits cancel each other.

  D. External magnetic fields cancel the fields inside network cabling.

11. Which of the following describes impedance in networking media?

  A. Impedance involves resistance and reactance to current caused by signal degradation.

  B. Electrical components in the NICs create impedance on the networking media.

  C. Signal degradation causes impedance.

  D. Networking media impedance needs to match the network interface card electrical components.

12. When can impedance degrade the signal in networking media?

  A. When resistance opposes reactance

  B. When cable impedance does not match network interface card electrical components

  C. When networking media is not properly shielded from EMI/RFI interference

  D. When cancellation techniques are not employed

13. Which of the following best describes *attenuation* ?

    A. The termination of a message

    B. The interception of a message

    C. The weakening of a message

    D. The ignoring of a message

14. Which of the following best describes how data is transmitted on a network?

    A. As hexadecimal code

    B. As ASCII text

    C. As 1s and 0s

    D. As voltage pulses

15. Which of the following best describes the states of digital signals?

    A. Alphanumeric

    B. Octets

    C. On or off

    D. Yes or no

16. What does the binary number 1 correspond to in a digital signal?

    A. On

    B. One

    C. The letter *A*

    D. Off

17. What does the binary number 0 correspond to in a digital signal?

    A. On

    B. One

    C. The letter *A*

    D. Off

18. Which best describes a *digital signal*?

    A. A sine wave of normal shape and amplitude

    B. An electrical technique used to convey binary signals

    C. A language of computers with only two states—on and off—which are indicated by a series of voltage pulses

    D. A transmission sent by a transceiver back to a controller to let it know the collision circuitry is functional

19. How do computers recognize digital signals?

    A. They receive a broadcast signal from the network.

    B. They look for ARP requests that match their IP address.

    C. They monitor the network connection for modulations.

    D. They measure and compare the signals to a reference point.

20. What is the signal reference ground?

    A. A neutral contact point where the computer chassis and the network connection meet

    B. A point that devices use to measure and compare incoming digital signals to

    C. A device that the name server uses to send messages over the network

    D. A ground that prevents users from receiving shocks when power fails

21. What is the point that a device uses to measure and compare incoming digital signals called?

    A. Input point

    B. Zero point

    C. Null reference setting

    D. Signal reference ground

22. How is the signal reference ground established?

    A. By connecting the ground wire to the network wire

    B. By connecting the network wire to the jumper connector

    C. By connecting the ground plane to the computer's cabinet

    D. By connecting the computer chassis to the network cable

23. What purpose does the computer chassis serve?

    A. It prevents electrical short circuits and electrical fires.

    B. It serves as signal reference ground and AC power-line ground.

    C. It amplifies digital signals.

    D. It reduces electromagnetic interference.

24. What is the most likely cause of interference on a network?

    A. Improper cabling and jack choices

    B. Electromagnetic interference from radios and other electrical devices

    C. High voltage device in the vicinity

    D. Problems with the power ground

25. What is the most likely cause of problems with the power ground?

    A. Length of the neutral and ground wires in electrical outlets

    B. Excessive stripping or untwisting of cable

    C. Equipment not located in a climate-controlled area

    D. Poor-quality cabling material used in the network

26. What do long neutral and ground wires in electrical outlets act as?

    A. Lightning rods

    B. Amplifiers for digital signals

    C. Antenna for electrical noise

    D. Line signal dampeners

27. How does electrical noise affect networks?

    A. It shuts down the network.

    B. It burns out network devices, especially hubs.

    C. It reduces data transmission speed through the network because error-trapping routines are initiated.

    D. It distorts or buries digital signals to the point that they become unrecognizable.

28. How can the problem of electrical noise be avoided?

    A. By limiting the number and type of electrical devices near the LAN

    B. By working closely with your electrical contractor and the local power company

    C. By making sure that all electrical devices are FCC and UL listed

    D. By installing surge suppressors on every network device

29. How can having a single power transformer dedicated to your LAN reduce electrical noise?

    A. You can detect and filter out fluctuations in line voltage before they reach your LAN.

    B. You can specify the size and capacity of the transformer.

    C. You can place the transformer in a central location.

    D. You can control how and where devices such as motors or high current devices are attached.

30. What is the unit of measure for electrical current?

    A. Volt

    B. Watt

    C. Amp

    D. Ohm

31. What type of fiber-optic cable is required by the TIA/EIA-568B standard for horizontal cabling?

    A. Two pairs of 100-ohm cable

    B. Two pairs of 150-ohm cable

    C. Two fibers of 62.5/125 um multimode cable

    D. Four fibers of 62.5/125 um multimode cable

32. How can you determine which category of UTP cable a cabling belongs to?

    A. By looking at the end connectors

    B. By reading the UL marking

    C. By measuring the cable diameter

    D. By the color of the cable sheathing

33. Why do networks need to use an access method?

    A. To regulate access to the networking media equitably

    B. To regulate the access of data into certain parts of networking media

    C. To keep unwanted, foreign users from having access to the network

    D. To prioritize data transmissions so that important items have greater access

34. Which of the following best describes an access method?

    A. The method that software uses to access network file servers

    B. The method that is used to verify users as authorized for access to the network

    C. The way that users access the network

    D. The way that network devices access the network medium

35. Ethernet uses what access method?

    A. Token header transmission protocol.

    B. Ethernet does not use an access method.

    C. Carrier sense multiple access collision detect.

    D. Ethernet transmission carrier collision detect.

36. Which of the following best describes a collision?

    A. The frames from two devices impact and are damaged when they meet on the physical media.

    B. Two nodes transmit at the same time and one data packet has priority, so it obliterates the lesser packet.

    C. Two data transmissions cross paths on the network media and corrupt each other.

    D. A data transmission is corrupted due to an energy spike over the network media.

37. Which of the following best describes a backoff algorithm?

    A. A process wherein the network holds up some data so that other, more important data can get through

    B. The retransmission delay that is enforced when a collision occurs

    C. The signal that a device on the network sends out to tell the other devices that data is being sent

    D. A mathematical function that networking software performs to prioritize data packets

38. What is most important when considering the type of networking media to use in an installation?

    A. Management's wishes

    B. Availability of networking media from local sources

    C. Applicable fire, building, and safety codes

    D. Your experience and expertise

39. Which grade of UTP cabling described in the TIA/EIA-568B standard is used for running CDDI and can transmit data at speeds up to 100 Mbps?

    A. Category 2

    B. Category 3

    C. Category 4

    D. Category 5

40. Which grade of UTP cabling described in the TIA/EIA-568B standard is the one most frequently recommended and implemented in installations today?

    A. Category 2

    B. Category 3

    C. Category 4

    D. Category 5

41. What is Category 5 UTP cabling suitable for?

    A. Transmitting data at speeds up to 10 Mbps

    B. Transmitting data at speeds up to 100 Mbps

    C. 10BASE-T networks

    D. Token Ring networks

42. What type of STP cable does the TIA/EIA-568B standard require for horizontal cabling?

    A. Two pairs of 100-ohm cable

    B. Two pairs of 150-ohm cable

    C. Four pairs of 100-ohm cable

    D. Four pairs of 150-ohm cable

43. What type of UTP cable does the TIA/EIA-568B standard require for horizontal cabling?

    A. Two pairs of 100-ohm cable

    B. Two pairs of 150-ohm cable

    C. Four pairs of 100-ohm cable

    D. Four pairs of 150-ohm cable

Cable Testing

This chapter describes issues relating to the testing of media used for physical layer connectivity in local-area networks (LANs). Networking media is literally and physically the backbone of a network. Inferior quality of network cabling results in network failures and in networks with unreliable performance. All three categories of networking media (copper-based, optical fiber, and wireless) require testing and measurement to determine its quality, and this testing is the subject of this chapter. The equipment used to perform these tests involves certain electrical and mathematical concepts and terms, such as signal, wave, frequency, and noise. Understanding this vocabulary is helpful when learning about networking, cabling, and cable testing.

Upon completion of this chapter, you will be able to

- Discuss the basic terminology used for frequency-based cable testing

- Explain what signals and noise impact networking media

Concept Questions

Demonstrate your knowledge of these concepts by answering the following questions in the space provided.

1. Networking professionals are interested in specific types of waves: voltage waves on copper media, light waves in optical fiber, and alternating electric and magnetic fields called electromagnetic waves. What is the difference between Sine waves and Square waves, and which one represents an analog or digital wave?

   _____

   _____

2. In networking, there are three important number systems: BASE 2 (binary), BASE 10 (decimal), and BASE 16 (hexadecimal). Recall that the base of a number system refers to the number of different symbols that can occupy one place. Describe the placeholder philosophy for these three number systems.

   _____

   _____

3. An important way of describing networking signals is a unit of measure called the decibel (dB). The decibel is related to the exponents and logarithms. The formulas for calculating decibels are as follows:

   $dB = 10 \log_{10} (P_{final} / P_{ref})$, or

   $dB = 20 \log_{10} (V_{final} / V_{reference})$

What do the following terms represent in these preceding formulas?

dB

$\log_{10}$

P_{final}

P_{ref}

V_{final}

V_{ref}

_____

_____

4. What is it called when you use an oscilloscope to analyze the x-axis or domain of the mathematical function over time?

_____

_____

5. All communications systems have noise. Even though you completely eliminate noise, you can minimize its effects if you understand the sources of the noise. What are some sources of noise?

_____

_____

6. Bandwidth is an extremely important concept in communications systems. There are two ways of considering bandwidth that are important for the study of LANs: analog bandwidth and digital bandwidth. Describe the differences between analog and digital bandwidth.

_____

_____

7. How does a fiber optic installation represent zeros and ones?

_____

_____

8. List and describe some of the factors that cause attenuation in copper media?

_____

_____

9. List and describe the tests that are specified by TIA/EIA 568B for copper cable?

_____

_____

10. Describe how crosstalk can be detected?

_____

_____

Vocabulary Exercise

Define the following terms as completely as you can. Use the online curriculum or CCNA 1 Chapter 4 from the *Cisco Networking Academy Program CCNA 1 and 2 Companion Guide*, Revised Third Edition, for help.

analog bandwidth

_____
_____

amplitude

_____
_____

attenuation

_____
_____

crosstalk

_____
_____

decibel

_____
_____

digital bandwidth

_____
_____

frequency

_____
_____

impedance mismatch

_____
_____

NEXT

_____
_____

oscilloscope

_____
_____

propagation delay

_____
_____

PSNEXT

_____
_____

sine waves

_____

_____

square waves

_____

_____

TIA/EIA-568-B standard

_____

_____

wave

_____

_____

white noise

_____

_____

Focus Questions

1. Which standards body created the cables and connector specification used to support Ethernet implementation?

    A. ISO

    B. ANSI

    C. EIA/TIA

    D. IETF

2. What equipment do you use to graph electrical waves, pulses, and patterns?

    _____

    _____

3. What are some of the characteristics of an analog signal?

    _____

    _____

CCNA Exam Review Questions

The following questions help you prepare for the CCNA exam. Answers appear in Appendix B, "CCNA 1 and 2 Exam Review Questions Answer Key."

1. Which of the following is an external source of degradation of the signal on cabling?

    A. EMI caused by electrical motors

    B. RFI caused by light leakage

    C. Impedance caused by radio systems

    D. RFI caused by lighting

2. Which of the following would increase attenuation in a long 10BASE-T cable run?

    A. Type of network traffic

    B. Length of cable

    C. Type of electrical ground

    D. Number of hosts connected to the segment

3. What is the cause of crosstalk?

    A. Cable wires that are too large in diameter

    B. Too much noise in a cable's data signal

    C. Electrical motors and lighting

    D. Electrical signals from other wires in a cable

4. How does crosstalk occur?

    A. Two wires are placed in close proximity to each other.

    B. Network interface cards fail to discriminate the noise from the data signal.

    C. Electrical noise originates from signals on other wires in the cable.

    D. Wires in a cable absorb electrical impulses from sources that are outside the cable.

5. What is a cost-effective way to limit cable signal degradation?

    A. Specify the maximum cable length between nodes.

    B. Increase the size of the conductors in the cabling.

    C. Improve the type of insulating material.

    D. Use a braid or foil covering on wires as a shield.

6. What is *cancellation* in networking media?

    A. The magnetic fields of same-circuit wires cancel each other.

    B. External magnetic fields cancel the fields inside network cabling.

    C. Wires in the same circuit cancel each other's electrical current flow.

    D. Twisting wire pairs cancels the electrical impedance in the wires.

7. Which of the following describes cancellation in cabling?

    A. Wires in the same circuit cancel each other's electrical current flow.

    B. Twisting wire pairs provides self-shielding within the network media.

    C. The magnetic fields of wires on different electrical circuits cancel each other.

    D. External magnetic fields cancel the fields inside network cabling.

8. Which of the following describes impedance in networking media?

    A. Impedance involves resistance and reactance to current that signal degradation causes.

    B. Electrical components in the network interface cards create impedance on the networking media.

    C. Signal degradation causes impedance.

    D. Networking media impedance needs to match the network interface card electrical components.

9. When can impedance degrade the signal in networking media?

    A. When resistance opposes reactance

    B. When cable impedance does not match network interface card electrical components

    C. When networking media is not properly shielded from EMI/RFI interference

    D. When cancellation techniques are not employed

10. Which of the following best describes *attenuation*?

    A. The termination of a message

    B. The interception of a message

    C. The weakening of a message

    D. The ignoring of a message

11. How is data transmitted on a network?

    A. As hexadecimal code

    B. As ASCII text

    C. As 1s and 0s

    D. As voltage pulses

12. Which of the following best describes the states of digital signals?

    A. Alphanumeric

    B. Octets

    C. On or off

    D. Yes or no

13. What does the binary number 1 correspond to in a digital signal?

    A. On

    B. One

    C. The letter *A*

    D. Off

14. What does the binary number 0 correspond to in a digital signal?

    A. On

    B. One

    C. The letter *A*

    D. Off

15. Which of the following best describes a digital signal?

    A. A sine wave of normal shape and amplitude

    B. An electrical technique that is used to convey binary signals

    C. A language of computers with only two states—on and off—that are indicated by a series of voltage pulses

    D. A transmission that a transceiver sends back to a controller to let it know the collision circuitry is functional

16. How do computers recognize digital signals?

    A. They receive a broadcast signal from the network.

    B. They look for ARP requests that match their IP address.

    C. They monitor the network connection for modulations.

    D. They measure and compare the signals to a reference point.

17. What is the signal reference ground?

    A. A neutral contact point where the computer chassis and the network connection meet

    B. A point that devices use to measure and compare incoming digital
       signals to

    C. A device that the name server uses to send messages over the network

    D. A ground that prevents users from receiving shocks when power fails

18. What is the point that a device uses to measure and compare incoming digital signals called?

    A. Input point

    B. Zero point

    C. Null reference setting

    D. Signal reference ground

19. How is the signal reference ground established?

    A. By connecting the ground wire to the network wire

    B. By connecting the network wire to the jumper connector

    C. By connecting the ground plane to the computer's cabinet

    D. By connecting the computer chassis to the network cable

20. What purpose does the computer chassis serve?

    A. It prevents electrical short circuits and electrical fires.

    B. It serves as signal reference ground and AC power-line ground.

    C. It amplifies digital signals.

    D. It reduces electromagnetic interference.

21. What is the most likely cause of problems with the power ground?

    A. Length of the neutral and ground wires in electrical outlets

    B. Excessive stripping or untwisting of cable

    C. Equipment not located in a climate-controlled area

    D. Poor-quality cabling material used in the network

22. What do long neutral and ground wires in electrical outlets act as?

    A. Lightning rods

    B. Amplifiers for digital signals

    C. Antenna for electrical noise

    D. Line signal dampeners

23. How does electrical noise affect networks?

    A. It shuts down the network.

    B. It burns out network devices, especially hubs.

    C. It reduces data transmission speed through the network because error-trapping routines are initiated.

    D. It distorts or buries digital signals to the point that they become unrecognizable.

24. How can the problem of electrical noise be avoided?

    A. By installing surge suppressors on every network device

    B. By making sure all electrical devices are FCC and UL listed

    C. By getting a single power transformer dedicated to your LAN

    D. By limiting the number and type of electrical devices near the LAN

25. Which is a reason for shielding copper based media?

    A. Ground the host.

    B. Protect the data from outside forces

    C. Decrease attenuation on the wire

    D. Increase the crosstalk on the wire.

26. For which frequency should cable always be tested?

    A. Highest frequency that the cable is rated to support

    B. Lowest frequency that the cable is rate to support

    C. 10 kHz in each direction

    D. 100 bps in each direction

Cabling LANs and WANs

This chapter describes issues related to cabling networking devices for a LAN and a WAN. For the LAN to function properly, the physical layer medium must meet the industry standards specified for the data rate used to transmit signals over Ethernet (10, 100, 1000, or 10,000 Mbps). The use of "signals" in this text refers to the data signals that move from the transmitter to the receiver. The signals will weaken (attenuate) traveling over the physical media; however, the receiver must still be able to clearly determine the state of each bit of the data (one or zero). Otherwise, the error rate on the network will be too high for the LAN to be useful.

Upon completion of this chapter, you will be able to

- Demonstrate how to cable a LAN
- Demonstrate how to cable a WAN

Vocabulary Exercise

Define the following terms as completely as you can. Use the online curriculum or CCNA 1 Chapter 5 from the *Cisco Networking Academy Program CCNA 1 and 2 Companion Guide*, Revised Third Edition, for help.

active hub

_____

_____

AUI

_____

_____

crossover cable

_____

_____

GBIC

_____

_____

IEEE 802.1X/EAP

_____

_____

intelligent hub

_____

_____

passive hub

_____

_____

peer-to-peer network

_____

_____

RJ-45

_____

_____

straight-through cable

_____

_____

WEP

_____

_____

Focus Questions

1. Which of the following is an 802.3u specification?

    A. 10BASE-F

    B. 10BASE-T

    C. 100BASE-TX

    D. 1000BASE-CX

2. Which of the following is the most appropriate choice for Ethernet connectivity?

    A. Use 10-Mbps Ethernet as a connection between server and LAN.

    B. Use Gigabit Ethernet as the link at the user level to provide good performance.

    C. Use Fast Ethernet as a link between the user level and network devices to support the aggregate traffic from each Ethernet segment on the access link.

    D. None of the above.

3. Which of the following statements does *not* correctly describe a media connector?

    A. An RJ-45 connector is an 8-pin connector that is used mainly to terminate coaxial cable.

    B. An AUI is a 15-pin connector that is used between a network interface card and an Ethernet cable.

    C. The GBIC is a transceiver that converts serial electric currents to optical signals, and vice versa.

    D. None of the above.

4. For which of the following would you *not* need to provide a crossover cable?

    A. Connecting uplinks between switches

    B. Connecting routers to switches

    C. Connecting hubs to switches

    D. None of the above

5. Which technology is *not* a type of wireless communication?

    A. Cellular

    B. Wideband

    C. Infrared

    D. Spread spectrum

6. Which statement does *not* describe the features of direct-sequence spread spectrum (DSSS)?

    A. DSSS is reliable because each bit is represented by a string of 1s and 0s.

    B. If up to 40 percent of the string is lost, you can reconstruct the original transmission.

    C. DSSS technology has low throughput of data and short-range access.

    D. The recently released evolution of the IEEE standard, 802.11b, provides for a full Ethernet-like data rate of 11 Mbps over DSSS.

7. Which of the following is *not* a feature of wired equivalent privacy (WEP)?

    A. WEP uses the RC4 stream cipher for encryption.

    B. WEP is a security mechanism defined within the 802.3 standards.

    C. One of the goals of WEP is to deny access to the network by unauthorized users who do not possess the appropriate WEP key.

    D. None of the above.

8. Which of the following is *not* a physical WAN implementation?

    A. DSL

    B. ISDN

    C. Frame Relay

    D. Ethernet

9. What type of data-transmission method does a WAN use?

    A. Parallel

    B. Serial

    C. Single

    D. None of above

10. What best describes a DCE?

   A. User device at the end of a network

   B. Equipment that serves as the data source or destination

   C. Physical devices such as protocol translators and multiplexers

   D. Devices that make up the network end of the user-to-network interface

11. Which of the following media is used to interconnect the ISDN BRI port to the service-provider device?

   A. Category 5 UTP straight-through

   B. Category 5 UTP crossover

   C. Coaxial

   D. Fiber optic

12. What type of connector is used for DSL connection?

   A. RJ-45

   B. RJ-11

   C. F

   D. DB-9

13. What type of connector is used to connect a router and a cable system?

   A. RJ-45

   B. RJ-11

   C. F

   D. AUI

14. What type of cable is used to connect a terminal and a console port?

   A. Straight-through

   B. Rollover

   C. Crossover

   D. Coaxial

CCNA Exam Review Questions

The following questions help you prepare for the CCNA exam. Answers appear in Appendix B, "CCNA 1 and 2 Exam Review Questions Answer Key."

1. Which of the following correctly describes the type of signal that the network media carries?

   A. Coaxial cable carries pulses of light.

   B. Unshielded twisted-pair (UTP) cable carries impedance signals.

   C. Shielded twisted-pair (STP) cable carries electrical impulses.

   D. Fiber-optic cable carries electrical impulses.

2. Which network media carries pulses of light?

    A. Coaxial cable

    B. Fiber-optic cable

    C. UTP cable

    D. STP cable

Ethernet Fundamentals

In this chapter, you learn about the history of Ethernet and IEEE Ethernet standards. This chapter discusses the operation of Ethernet, Ethernet framing, error handling, and the different type of collisions on Ethernet networks. In addition, this chapter introduces the collision domains and broadcast domains. Finally, this chapter describes segmentation and the devices used to create the network segments.

Concept Questions

Demonstrate your knowledge of these concepts by answering the following questions in the space provided.

1. The IEEE is a professional organization that defines network standards. In 1985, the IEEE standards committee for local and metropolitan networks published its standards for LANs. Describe some of the purposes of this organization.

   _____

   _____

2. An abbreviated description (called an *identifier*) is also assigned to the supplement. The following are examples of some of the supplements:

   ■ 10BASE-2

   ■ 10BASE-5

   ■ 100BASE-T

   ■ 1000BASE-TX

   What do these abbreviated descriptions consist of?

   _____

   _____

3. LAN standards define the physical media and the connectors that are used to connect devices to media at the physical layer of the OSI reference model. LAN standards also define the way devices communicate at the data link layer. In addition, LAN standards define how to encapsulate protocol-specific traffic. To provide these functions, the IEEE Ethernet data link layer has two sublayers. What are these layers, and what purposes do they serve?

   _____

   _____

4. To allow for local delivery of frames on an Ethernet segment, there must be an addressing system and a way of naming the computers and interfaces. Every computer has a unique way of identifying itself. Each computer on a network has a physical address. No two physical addresses on a network should be alike. Referred to as the MAC address, the

physical address is located on the network interface card. Explain how Ethernet uses the MAC address, and define what the parts of the MAC address represent.

_____

_____

5. All frames (and the bits, bytes, and fields that are contained within them) are susceptible to errors from a variety of sources. The frame check sequence (FCS) field contains a number that is calculated by the source computer and is based on the data in the frame. When the destination computer receives the frame, it recalculates the FCS number and compares it to the FCS number included in the frame. If the two numbers are different, an error is assumed, the frame is discarded, and the source is asked to retransmit.

There are three primary ways to calculate the Frame Check Sequence number. List and describe these three methods.

_____

_____

6. Ethernet is a shared-media broadcast technology. The access method used in Ethernet is CSMA/CD. List and describe the three functions the CSMA/CD access method performs. Also describe how the CSMA/CD access method works.

_____

_____

7. Which companies were responsible for the first Ethernet LAN specification? (Remember DIX).

_____

_____

8. Describe the four repeater rule below

_____

_____

9. Describe 2B1D with ISDN below

_____

_____

10. Compare and contrast the peer-to-peer network model to the client/server model

_____

_____

Vocabulary Exercise

Define the following terms as completely as you can. Use the online curriculum or CCNA 1 Chapter 6 from the *Cisco Networking Academy Program CCNA 1 and 2 Companion Guide*, Revised Third Edition, for help.

10 Gigabit-Ethernet

_____

_____

auxiliary port

_____

_____

backoff

_____

_____

broadcast

_____

_____

broadcast domain

_____

_____

collision

_____

_____

collision domain

_____

_____

connectionless

_____

_____

CSMA/CD

_____

_____

CSU/DSU

_____

_____

DCE

_____

_____

encapsulation

_____

_____

Ethernet

_____

_____

Fast Ethernet

_____

_____

FDDI

_____

_____

full duplex

_____

_____

Gigabit Ethernet

_____

_____

half duplex

_____

_____

header

_____

_____

IEEE

_____

_____

IEEE 802.2

_____

_____

IEEE 802.3

_____

_____

ISDN

_____

_____

LLC

_____

_____

MAC

_____

_____

MAC address

_____

_____

MTU

_____

_____

OUI

_____

_____

PPP

_____

_____

propagation delay

_____

_____

segment

_____

_____

RJ-45

_____

_____

simplex

_____

_____

SNMP

_____

_____

Token Ring

_____

_____

trailer

_____

_____

transceiver

_____

_____

Focus Questions

1. Which of the following is *not* one of the recognized IEEE sublayers?

   A. MAC

   B. Data Link Control

   C. Logical Link Control

   D. None of the above

2. The recognized IEEE sublayers are concerned with what layers of the OSI reference model?

   A. 2 and 3

   B. 1 and 2

   C. 3 and 4

   D. 1 and 3

3. The LLC, as a sublayer, participates in which of the following processes?

   A. Encryption

   B. Encapsulation

   C. Framing

   D. All of the above

4. What do the first six hexadecimal numbers in a MAC address represent?

   A. Interface serial number

   B. Organizational unique identifier

   C. Interface unique identifier

   D. None of the above

5. MAC addresses are _____ bits in length.

   A. 12

   B. 24

   C. 48

   D. 64

6. What is the name of the method used in Ethernet that explains how Ethernet works?

   A. TCP/IP

   B. CSMA/CD

   C. CMDA/CS

   D. CSMA/CA

7. Where does the MAC address reside?

    A. Transceiver

    B. Computer BIOS

    C. Network interface card

    D. CMOS

8. Which of the following statements best describes communication between two devices on a LAN?

    A. The source device encapsulates data in a frame with the MAC address of the destination device and then transmits it. Everyone on the LAN sees it, but the devices that have nonmatching addresses otherwise ignore the frame.

    B. The source encapsulates the data and places a destination MAC address in the frame. It puts the frame on the LAN, where only the device that has the matching address can check the address field.

    C. The destination device encapsulates data in a frame with the MAC address of the source device, puts it on the LAN, and the device that has the matching address removes the frame.

    D. Each device on the LAN receives the frame and passes it up to the computer, where software decides whether to keep or to discard the frame.

9. Which functions are associated with framing?

    A. Identification of which computers are communicating with one another

    B. Signaling when communication between individual computers begins and when it ends

    C. Flagging corrupted frames

    D. All of the above

10. How does a computer on a LAN detect an error in a frame?

    A. It sends a copy of the frame back to the sender for verification.

    B. It checks the destination address to verify that the frame was really intended for it.

    C. It compares a frame check sequence (FCS) in the frame to one that the computer calculates from the contents of the frame.

    D. It calculates a checksum from the data in the frame and then sends it back to the source for verification.

11. What does MAC refer to?

    A. The state in which a network interface card has captured the networking media and is ready to transmit

    B. Rules that govern media capturing and releasing

    C. Protocols that determine which computer on a shared-medium environment is allowed to transmit the data

    D. A formal byte sequence that has been transmitted

12. Which best describes a CSMA/CD network?

    A. One node's transmission traverses the entire network and is received and examined by every node.

    B. Signals are sent directly to the destination if the source knows both the MAC and IP addresses.

    C. One node's transmission goes to the nearest router, which sends it directly to the destination.

    D. Signals are always sent in broadcast mode.

13. In an Ethernet or IEEE 802.3 LAN, when do collisions occur?

    A. When one node places a packet on a network without informing the other nodes

    B. When two stations listen for traffic, hear none, and transmit simultaneously

    C. When two network nodes send packets to a node that is no longer broadcasting

    D. When jitter is detected and traffic is disrupted during normal transmission

14. Which of the following is an important Layer 2 data link layer function?

    A. Logical link control

    B. Addressing

    C. MAC

    D. All of the above

15. Which of the following is an Ethernet frame error type?

    A. Local collision

    B. Remote collision

    C. Late collision

    D. All of the above

16. Which of the following protocols is a nondeterministic protocol?

    A. Token Ring

    B. CSMA/CD

    C. IPX

    D. RIP

17. Which of the following is true of a deterministic MAC protocol?

    A. It defines collisions and specifies what to do about them.

    B. It allows the hub to determine the number of users who are active at any one time.

    C. It allows hosts to "take turns" sending data.

    D. It allows network administrators to use a "talking stick" to control the media access of any users who are considered troublemakers.

18. What is the network area within which data packets originate and collide?

    A. Collision domain

    B. Network domain

    C. Broadcast domain

    D. Network segment

19. Which of the following best describes broadcasting?

    A. Sending a single frame to many stations at the same time

    B. Sending a single frame to all routers to simultaneously update their routing tables

    C. Sending a single frame to all routers at the same time

    D. Sending a single frame to all hubs and bridges at the same time

20. Using repeaters _____ the collision domain.

    A. Reduces

    B. Has no effect on

    C. Extends

    D. None of the above

21. What is the process of using the complex networking devices—such as bridges, switches, and routers—to break up the collision domains known as?

    A. Sectioning

    B. Segmentation

    C. Collision domain reduction

    D. None of the above

22. Which of the following best describes a backoff algorithm?

    A. A process wherein the network holds up some data so that other, more important data can get through

    B. The retransmission delay that is enforced when a collision occurs

    C. The signal that a device on the network sends out to tell the other devices that data is being sent

    D. A mathematical function performed by networking software that prioritizes data packets

23. What are three differences between layer 1 and layer 2?

    _____

    _____

    _____

CCNA Exam Review Questions

The following questions help you prepare for the CCNA exam. Answers appear in Appendix B, "CCNA 1 and 2 Exam Review Questions Answer Key."

1. Why do networks need to use an access method?

    A. To regulate access to the networking media equitably

    B. To regulate the access of data to certain parts of networking media

    C. To keep unwanted, foreign users from having access to the network

    D. To prioritize data transmissions so that important items have greater access

2. Which of the following would not use a crossover cable?

    A. Router to a switch

    B. Workstation to a hub

    C. Switch to a workstation

    D. All of the above

3. Ethernet uses which of the following access methods?

    A. Token header transmission protocol.

    B. Ethernet does not use an access method.

    C. CSMA/CD.

    D. Ethernet transmission carrier collision detect.

4. Which of the following best describes a collision?

    A. The frames from two devices impact and are damaged when they meet on the physical media.

    B. Two nodes transmit at the same time and one data packet has priority, so it obliterates the lesser packet.

    C. Two data transmissions cross paths on the network media and corrupt each other.

    D. A data transmission is corrupted due to an energy spike over the network media.

5. Where do all communications on a network originate?

    A. Peripherals

    B. Sources

    C. Computers

    D. Hosts

6. Which layer of the OSI model is concerned with media?

    A. Transport

    B. Network

    C. Physical

    D. Application

7. What is a source device?

    A. A source device receives data and information from other computers in a network.

    B. A source device sends data and information to other computers in a network.

    C. A source device is information that moves among computers in a network.

    D. A source device provides connectivity among computers in a network.

8. What layer 2 protocol is typically used with ISDN?

    A. HDLC

    B. FRF8

    C. ATM

    D. PPP

9. Which of the following best defines a destination?

    A. Logically grouped units of information

    B. A network device that is receiving data

    C. A redundant use of equipment to prevent data loss

    D. A network device that is sending data

10. What is another name for link layer addresses?

    A. MAC addresses

    B. IP addresses

    C. Logical addresses

    D. Network addresses

11. Which of the following is not a type of hub?

    A. Active

    B. Intelligent

    C. Passive

    D. Transparent

12. On which layer of the OSI model are physical addresses located?

    A. On the presentation layer

    B. On the session layer

    C. On the data link layer

    D. On the network layer

13. Which of the following is true about MAC addresses?

    A. They are unique for each LAN interface.

    B. They are located at the network layer.

    C. They are also called logical addresses.

    D. They identify host networks.

14. Where is the MAC address located?

    A. At the network layer

    B. Burned into ROM at the factory

    C. In the AUI

    D. At the MAU interface

15. Which of the following describes the structure of a MAC address?

    A. 32-bit network identity plus 32-bit host identity

    B. Network, subnet, subnet mask, host

    C. 24-bit vendor code plus 24-bit serial number

    D. Network code plus serial number

16. Which of the following could be a MAC address?

    A. 172.15.5.31

    B. 1111.1111.111

    C. FFFF.FFFF.FFFF

    D. 0000.0c12.3456

17. Which of the following best describes CSMA/CD?

    A. Devices check the channel to make sure no signals are being sent before transmitting data.

    B. Devices transmit data and listen to make sure that they are received properly.

    C. Devices transmit a request prior to transmitting data over the network and wait for an "all clear" reply.

    D. Devices monitor the channel continuously to track and manage traffic.

18. Which of the following is *not* a function of CSMA/CD?

    A. Transmitting and receiving data packets

    B. Decoding data packets and checking them for valid addresses

    C. Detecting errors within data packets or on the network

    D. Cleaning up collisions on the network medium

Ethernet Technologies

Ethernet and its associated IEEE 802.3 protocols are part of the world's most important networking standards. Because of the great success of the original Ethernet and the soundness of its design, it has evolved over time. This evolution was in response to the developing needs of modern LANs. It is likely that Ethernet will continue to evolve in response to future demands for network capability.

In Chapter 6, "Ethernet Fundamentals," you were introduced to both the history of Ethernet and the standards associated with it. You also learned that the term *Ethernet* refers to a family of Ethernet technologies. This chapter discusses the Ethernet technologies in more detail.

Concept Questions

Demonstrate your knowledge of these concepts by answering the following questions in the space provided.

1. One process that is particularly important at the physical layer level is the signal quality error (SQE) signal. This signal is typical of something we will see in many networking technologies. At the physical layer, the network is "alive" with communications other than our user data to ensure a properly functioning network. SQE is always used in half duplex; it is not required but is permitted in full-duplex operation. What are the reasons for SQE being active?

2. Describe the 5-4-3 rule.

3. What are some reasons to use 100BASE-FX (introduced as part of the 802.3u-1995 standard) as opposed to other Ethernet standards?

4. Ethernet, Fiber Distributed Data Interface (FDDI), and Token Ring are widely used LAN technologies that account for virtually all deployed LANs. LAN standards specify cabling and signaling at the physical and data link layers of the OSI model. Because they are widely adhered to, this book covers the Ethernet and IEEE 802.3 LAN standards. Why do you suppose that Ethernet technology is so heavily used?

5. When it was developed, Ethernet was designed to fill the middle ground between long-distance, low-speed networks and specialized, computer-room networks carrying data at high speeds for limited distances. Ethernet is well suited to applications in which a local communication medium must carry sporadic, occasionally heavy traffic at high-peak data rates. Why is Ethernet so well suited to this kind of traffic?

_____

_____

_____

6. Today, the term *standard Ethernet* refers to all networks using Ethernet (a shared-medium technology) that generally conform to Ethernet specifications, including IEEE 802.3. To use this shared-medium technology, Ethernet uses the carrier sense multiple access collision detect (CSMA/CD) protocol to allow the networking devices to negotiate for the right to transmit. Describe the CSMA/CD functions?

_____

_____

_____

Vocabulary Exercise

Define the following terms as completely as you can. Use the online curriculum or CCNA 1 Chapter 7 from the *Cisco Networking Academy Program CCNA 1 and 2 Companion Guide*, Revised Third Edition, for help.

4D-PAM5

_____

_____

8B1Q4

_____

_____

10BASE-2

_____

_____

10BASE-5

_____

_____

10BASE-T

_____

_____

100BASE-FX

_____

_____

100BASE-TX

_____

_____

1000BASE-LX

_____

_____

1000BASE-SX

_____

_____

1000BASE-T

_____

_____

Focus Questions

1. What are the field names in a generic frame?

_____

_____

2. What happens on an Ethernet network after a collision occurs?

_____

_____

3. What address information is found in a layer 2 frame?

_____

_____

4. What are the features of Token Ring?

_____

_____

5. What are three advantages that optical fiber has over copper wiring?

_____

_____

6. What network device must all network traffic pass through on a star topology?

_____

_____

7. What factors led to the widespread growth of Ethernet networks?

_____

_____

8. What is the maximum distance for thick Ethernet without using a repeater?

   A. 185 m (606.95 feet)

   B. 250 m (820.2 feet)

   C. 500 m (1640.4 feet)

   D. 800 m (2624.64 feet)

9. 10 Mbps Ethernet operates within the timing limits offered by a series of not more than _____ segments separated by no more than _____ repeaters.

   A. Three, two

   B. Four, three

   C. Five, four

   D. Six, five

10. Fast Ethernet supports up to what transfer rate?

   A. 5 Mbps

   B. 10 Mbps

   C. 100 Mbps

   D. 1000 Mbps

11. Identify two Gigabit Ethernet cable specifications.

   A. 1000BASE-TX

   B. 1000BASE-FX

   C. 1000BASE-CS

   D. 1000BASE-LX

   E. 1000BASE-X

12. What is the transmission medium for 1000BASE-SX?

   A. Long-wave laser over single-mode and multimode fiber

   B. Category 5 UTP copper wiring

   C. Balanced, shielded, 150 ohm, two-pair STP copper cable

   D. Short-wave laser over multimode fiber

13. 4D-PAM5 encoding is used in which of the following Gigabit Ethernet standards?

   A. 1000BASE-LX

   B. 1000BASE-SX

   C. 1000BASE-T

   D. 1000BASE-CX

14. What is the IEEE standard for 10-Gigabit Ethernet?

   A. 802.3z

   B. 802.3u

   C. 802.3ae

   D. 803.3

Ethernet Switching

This chapter introduces Layer 2 bridging and switching techniques. Switching and bridging are techniques that decrease congestion in LANs by reducing traffic and increasing bandwidth. Three switching modes can be used to forward a frame through a switch: store-and-forward, cut-through, and fragment-free switching. The latency of each switching mode depends on how the switch forwards the frames. The faster the switching mode is, the smaller the latency is in the switch. Finally, this chapter introduces the Spanning Tree Protocol (STP), tells how STP works, and covers the STP switch port states.

Vocabulary Exercise

Define the following terms as completely as you can. Use the online curriculum or CCNA 1 Chapter 8 from the *Cisco Networking Academy Program CCNA 1 and 2 Companion Guide*, Revised Third Edition, for help.

BPDU

_____

_____

cut-through switching

_____

_____

encoding

_____

_____

fragment-free switching

_____

_____

latency

_____

_____

LLC

_____

_____

Manchester encoding

_____

_____

Media Access Control

_____

_____

microsegmentation

_____

_____

NRZ

_____

_____

NRZI

_____

_____

SNR

_____

_____

spanning tree

_____

_____

store-and-forward switching

_____

_____

STP

_____

_____

WDM

_____

_____

Focus Questions

1. What are two reasons that LANs are segmented?

_____

_____

_____

2. Ethernet uses which access method to detect errors within data packets or on the network?

_____

_____

_____

3. What is the name of the method used in Ethernet that explains how Ethernet works?

    A. TCP/IP

    B. CSMA/CD

    C. CMDA/CS

    D. CSMA/CA

4. Which of the following do LAN switches use to make the forwarding decision?

    A. IP address

    B. MAC address

    C. Network address

    D. Host address

5. Which of the following is a feature of full-duplex transmission?

    A. It offers two 10- to 1-Gbps data-transmission paths.

    B. It doubles bandwidth between nodes.

    C. It provides collision-free transmission.

    D. All of the above.

6. The three common types of switching methods are _____, _____, and _____.

7. The STP allows which of the following?

    A. Bridges to communicate Layer 3 information

    B. A redundant network path without suffering the effects of loops in the network

    C. Static network paths for loop prevention

    D. None of the above

8. Which of the following is *not* one of the STP port states?

    A. Blocking

    B. Learning

    C. Listening

    D. Transmitting

9. Which of the following is true concerning a bridge and its forwarding decisions?

    A. Bridges operate at OSI Layer 2 and use IP addresses to make decisions.

    B. Bridges operate at OSI Layer 3 and use IP addresses to make decisions.

    C. Bridges operate at OSI Layer 2 and use MAC addresses to make decisions.

    D. Bridges operate at OSI Layer 3 and use MAC addresses to make decisions.

10. Which of the following is *not* a feature of bridges?

    A. They operate at Layer 2 of the OSI model.

    B. They are more intelligent than hubs.

    C. They do not make forwarding decisions.

    D. They build and maintain address tables.

11. Which of the following statements is true of microsegmentation?

    A. Each workstation gets its own dedicated segment through the network.

    B. All the workstations are grouped as one segment.

    C. Microsegmentation increases the number of collisions on a network.

    D. None of the above.

12. Which of the following is true for LAN switches?

    A. They repair network fragments known as microsegments.

    B. They are high-speed multiport bridges.

    C. Lower bandwidth makes up for higher latency.

    D. They require new network interface cards on attached hosts.

CCNA Exam Review Questions

The following questions help you prepare for the CCNA exam. Answers appear in Appendix B, "CCNA 1 and 2 Exam Review Questions Answer Key."

1. Which of the following best describes the data link layer of the OSI model?

    A. It transmits data to other network layers.

    B. It provides services to application processes.

    C. It takes weak signals, cleans them, amplifies them, and sends them on their way across the network.

    D. It provides reliable transit of data across a physical link.

2. Which layer provides reliable transit of data across a physical link?

    A. Data link

    B. Physical

    C. Application

    D. Transport

3. Which of the following processes is the data link layer concerned with?

   A. Physical addressing, network topology, line discipline, error notification, ordered delivery of frames, and flow control

   B. Establishing, managing, and terminating sessions between applications and managing data exchange between presentation layer entities

   C. Synchronizing cooperating applications and establishing agreement on procedures for error recovery and control of data integrity

   D. Providing mechanisms for the establishment, maintenance, and termination of virtual circuits, transport fault detection, recovery, and information flow control

4. Physical addressing and network topology are handled by which layer?

   A. Physical

   B. Presentation

   C. Data link

   D. Session

5. On a network, where does a device connect to the media?

   A. Ethernet card

   B. Hub

   C. Router

   D. Network interface card

6. What is another name for the MAC address?

   A. Binary address

   B. Octadecimal address

   C. Physical address

   D. TCP/IP address

7. In which layer is the MAC address located?

   A. Session

   B. Data link

   C. Physical

   D. Transport

8. What does MAC address stand for?

   A. Macintosh Access Capable

   B. Mainframe Advisory Council

   C. Media Access Control

   D. Machine Application Communication

9. Which of the following items is located in the data link layer?

   A. Destination

   B. Peripheral

   C. Repeater

   D. MAC address

10. What is required for every port or device that connects to a network?

    A. Repeater

    B. Termination

    C. MAC or physical address

    D. ATM switch

11. Which of the following best describes MAC addressing?

    A. Addresses reside in the network interface card and the manufacturers assign them.

    B. The IEEE committee assigns addresses and the network administrator must request them.

    C. The distance of the computer from the network hub determines addresses.

    D. Addresses are given to every computer when it is manufactured.

12. How does a source device locate the destination for data on a network?

    A. The network interface card at the destination identifies its MAC address in a data packet.

    B. A data packet stops at the destination.

    C. The network interface card at the destination sends its MAC address to the source.

    D. The source sends a unique data packet to each MAC address on the network.

13. Which of the following has twelve hexadecimal digits?

    A. IP address

    B. MAC address

    C. SNAP address

    D. SAP address

TCP/IP Protocol Suite and IP Addressing

This chapter presents an overview of the TCP/IP Protocol Suite. It starts with the history and future of TCP/IP, compares the TCP/IP protocol model to the OSI reference model, and identifies and describes each layer of the TCP/IP protocol suite.

The U.S. Department of Defense (*DoD*) created the TCP/IP reference model because it wanted a network that could survive any conditions, even a nuclear war. To illustrate further, imagine a world at war, criss-crossed by different kinds of connections, such as wires, microwaves, optical fibers, and satellite links. Then imagine a need for data to be transmitted, regardless of the condition of any particular node or network on the internetwork (which, in this case, might have been destroyed by the war). The DoD wants its packets to get through every time, under any conditions, from any one point to any other point. This difficult design problem brought about the creation of the TCP/IP model and has since become the standard on which the Internet has grown.

The present version of TCP/IP is old. IPv4 was standardized in September 1981. In 1992, the Internet Engineering Task Force (IETF) supported the standardization of a new generation of IP, often called IPng. IPng is now known as IPv6. IPv6 has not yet gained wide implementation, but most vendors of networking equipment have already released it, and it will become the dominant standard in the future.

Concept Questions

1. IPv6 is the latest version of the TCP/IP protocol. What are some of the important IPv6 requirements?

   _____

   _____

2. What does the application layer provide in the TCP/IP protocol suite model?

   _____

   _____

3. What does the transport layer provide in the TCP/IP protocol suite model?

   _____

   _____

4. What does the Internet layer provide in the TCP/IP protocol suite model?

   _____

   _____

5. What does the network access layer provide in the TCP/IP protocol suite model?

_____

_____

6. Compare the OSI reference model to the TCP/IP model and discuss the similarities and differences.

_____

_____

7. Describe the major advantages of DHCP over BOOTP

_____

_____

Vocabulary Exercise

Define the following terms as completely as you can. Use the online curriculum or CCNA 1 Chapter 9 from the *Cisco Networking Academy Program CCNA 1 and 2 Companion Guide*, Revised Third Edition, for help.

application layer

_____

_____

BOOTP

_____

_____

broadcast address

_____

_____

Class A address

_____

_____

Class B address

_____

_____

Class C address

_____

_____

Class D address

_____

_____

Class E address

_____

_____

DHCP

_____

_____

ICMP

_____

_____

Internet layer

_____

_____

IP address classes

_____

_____

IPv6

_____

_____

multicast address

_____

_____

network access layer

_____

_____

subnetting

_____

_____

TCP/IP

_____

_____

transport layer

_____

_____

Focus Questions

1. The Class D address class was created to enable _____ in an IP network.

2. IP _____ is a bandwidth-conserving technology that reduces traffic by _____ delivering a single stream of information to thousands of corporate recipients and homes.

3. Complete the address chart that follows.

Address Class	First Octet Range	Number of Possible Networks	Number of Hosts Per Network
Class ___	0 to ___	_____ (2 are reserved)	
Class ___	___ to 191		
Class ___	192 to ___		

4. Fill in the class of address indicated by the network and host octets.

Class ____	Network		Host	
Octet	1	2	3	4

_____

Class ____	Network	Host		
Octet	1	2	3	4

_____

Class ____	Host			
Octet	1	2	3	4

_____

Class ____	Network			Host
Octet	1	2	3	4

_____

5. Two benefits of hierarchical addressing are _____ and _____ number of _____.

6. Three key features were invaluable in staving off depletion of the IPv4 address space. These features are the following:

   1) The replacement of _____ addressing by _____

   2) Enhanced route_____

   3) _____

7. Eliminating _____ wouldn't necessarily recover the addresses locked into those address spaces that were already assigned, but it would enable the remaining addresses to be used much more _____.

8. Classless interdomain routing (CIDR) enables Internet routers (or any CIDR-compliant router) to more efficiently _____ routing information. In other words, a single entry in a routing table can represent the address spaces of many _____.

9. _____ is nothing more than using _____ blocks of Class ___ address spaces to simulate a single, albeit larger address space.

10. Each CIDR-compliant network address is advertised with a _____.

11. _____, which is the next-generation IP, introduces a _____-bit address.

12. Five solutions to slow the depletion of IP addresses and to reduce the number of Internet route table entries by enabling more hierarchical layers in an IP address are as follows:

    1) _____ --- RFC 950 (1985); 1812 (1995).

    2) _____ ---RFC 1009 (1987). Allows the network designer to utilize multiple address schemes within a given class of address. You can use this strategy only when it is supported by the routing protocol, such as OSPF or EIGRP.

    3) _____ --- RFC 1918 (1996). Developed for organizations that do not need much access to the Internet.

    4) _____ --- RFC 1631 (1994). Developed for those companies that use private addressing or use non-network interface card-assigned IP addresses. This

    strategy enables an organization to access the Internet with a network interface card-assigned address without having to reassign the private or "illegal" addresses that are already in place.

    5) _____ ---RFCs 1518 and 1519 (1993). This is another method used for and developed for ISPs. This strategy suggests that the remaining IP addresses be allocated to ISPs in contiguous blocks, with geography being a consideration.

13. _____ provide the capability to include more than one subnet mask within a class-based address and the capability to subnet an _____.

14. VLSMs can be used when the routing protocol sends a _____ along with each network address. The protocols that support subnet mask information include _____, _____, _____, _____, _____, and _____.

15. Route summarization, also called *route* _____ or _____, reduces the number of routes that a router must maintain because it represents a series of network numbers as a single summary address.

16. Route summarization reduces memory use on routers, CPU for recalculations, and routing-protocol network traffic. Requirements for summarization to work correctly are as follows:

    Multiple IP addresses must share the same _____.

    _____ and _____ must base their routing decisions on a 32-bit IP address and prefix length that can be up to 32 bits.

    Routing protocols must carry the _____ (subnet mask) with the 32-bit IP address.

17. _____ and _____ do not advertise subnets or support noncontiguous subnets.

18. _____ and _____ are the two transport layer protocols.

19. Complete the following chart of private addresses. In the column on the right, give the network address with the CIDR prefix.

Class	RFC 1918 Internal Address Range	CIDR Prefix
	10.0.0.0 to _____	
	_____ to _____	
	_____ to _____	

20. The _____ router translates the internal local addresses into globally unique IP addresses before sending packets to the outside network.

21. _____ is also used for security reasons to hide internal _____.

22. Cisco IOS Software Release 11.2 and later supports the following additional NAT features:

    _____ —Establishes a one-to-one mapping between inside local and global addresses.

    _____ —Establishes a dynamic mapping between the inside local and global addresses. You accomplish dynamic mapping by describing the local addresses to be _____ and the _____ of addresses from which to allocate global addresses and associating the two. The _____ will create translations as needed.

    _____ —You can conserve addresses in the inside global address pool by allowing source _____ in TCP connections or UDP conversations to be translated. When different inside local addresses map to the same inside global address, each inside host's TCP or UDP _____ _____ are used to distinguish between them.

    _____ _____ —A dynamic form of destination translation can be configured for some outside-to-inside traffic. After a mapping is set up, destination addresses that match an access list are replaced with an address from a rotary pool. Allocation is done on a _____ basis, and only when a new connection is opened from the outside to the inside.

23. A_____ refers to a route whose associated mask has all 32 bits set to 1 --- 255.255.255.255. For an address and mask such as this, there can be only one host.

24. When you are troubleshooting IP unnumbered problems, always check the_____ _____ command from the interface that is providing the address.

25. Which two OSI model layers match the TCP/IP model network layer?

    _____

    _____

26. Why is IP an unreliable protocol?

    _____

    _____

CCNA Exam Review Questions

The following questions help you prepare for the CCNA exam. Answers appear in Appendix B, "CCNA 1 and 2 Exam Review Questions Answer Key."

1. Which transport layer protocol does TFTP use?

    A. TCP

    B. IP

    C. UDP

    D. CFTP

2. Which of the following is a basic service of the transport layer?

   A. Provide reliability by using sequence numbers and acknowledgments

   B. Segment upper-layer application data

   C. Establish end-to-end operations

   D. All of the above

3. Which of the following protocols operates at the TCP/IP Internet layer?

   A. IP

   B. ICMP

   C. ARP

   D. All of the above

4. What is the first thing that happens when a DHCP clients boots?

   A. DHCPREQUEST

   B. DHCPBOOT

   C. DHCPDISCOVER

   D. None of the above

5. How does the network layer forward packets from the source toward the destination?

   A. By using a routing table

   B. By using ARP responses

   C. By referring to a name server

   D. By referring to the bridge

6. If a device doesn't know the MAC address of a device on an adjacent network, what does it send an ARP request to?

   A. The default gateway

   B. The closest router

   C. The router interface

   D. All of the above

7. Which one of the following is not a method to expand the number if IP addresses available for public use?

   A. A 64-bit addressing scheme

   B. CIDR

   C. NAT

   D. IPv6

8. What are the two parts of an IP?

   A. Network address and host address

   B. Network address and MAC address

   C. Host address and MAC address

   D. MAC address and subnet mask

9. Which Internet protocol is used to map an IP address to a MAC address?

   A. UDP

   B. ICMP

   C. ARP

   D. RARP

10. Which of the following initiates an ARP request?

    A. A device that cannot locate the destination IP address in its ARP table

    B. The RARP server, in response to a malfunctioning device

    C. A diskless workstation that has an empty cache

    D. A device that cannot locate the destination MAC address in its ARP table

11. Which of the following best describes an ARP table?

    A. A method to reduce network traffic by providing lists of shortcuts and routes to common destinations

    B. A way to route data within networks that are divided into subnetworks

    C. A protocol that performs an application layer conversion of information from one stack to another

    D. A section of RAM on each device that maps IP addresses to MAC addresses

12. Which of the following best describes the ARP reply?

    A. The process of a device sending its MAC address to a source in response to an ARP request

    B. The route of the shortest path between the source and the destination

    C. The updating of ARP tables through intercepting and reading messages that are traveling on the network

    D. The method of finding IP addresses based on the MAC address, used primarily by RARP servers

13. Why are current, updated ARP tables important?

    A. For testing links in the network

    B. For limiting the amount of broadcasts

    C. For reducing network administrator maintenance time

    D. For resolving addressing conflicts

14. Which of the following is a function of ICMP?

    A. It provides name resolution services.

    B. It provides error messages for troubleshooting IP networks.

    C. It allows the network administrator to message users.

    D. It controls the flow of information between two routers.

15. Class A addresses begin with what two bits? (Choose two)

    A. The first bits of the binary address are always 00

    B. The first bits of the binary address are always 01

    C. The first bits of the binary address are always 10

    D. The first bits of the binary address are always 11

16. Which of the following best describes TCP/IP?

    A. It is a suite of protocols that can be used to communicate across any set of interconnected networks.

    B. It is a suite of protocols that allows LANs to connect into WANs.

    C. It is a suite of protocols that allows for data transmission across a multitude of networks.

    D. It is a suite of protocols that allows different devices to be shared by interconnected networks.

17. Which of the following does not describe the TCP/IP protocol stack?

    A. It maps closely to the OSI reference model's upper layers.

    B. It supports all standard physical and data link protocols.

    C. It transfers information in a sequence of datagrams.

    D. It reassembles datagrams into complete messages at the receiving location.

18. The TCP/IP protocol suite has specifications for which layer(s) of the OSI reference model?

    A. 1 through 3

    B. 1 through 4 and 7

    C. 3, 4, and 5 through 7

    D. 1, 3, and 4

19. Which of the following is *not* a function of the network layer?

    A. RARP determines network addresses when data link layer addresses are known.

    B. ICMP provides control and messaging capabilities.

    C. ARP determines the data link layer address for known IP addresses.

    D. UDP provides connectionless exchanges of datagrams without acknowledgments.

20. Which of the following is not a function of IP?

   A. Routing packets to remote hosts

   B. Transferring data between the data link layer and the transport layer

   C. Defining packets

   D. Defining frames

21. Which of the following is one of the protocols found at the transport layer?

   A. UCP

   B. UDP

   C. TDP

   D. TDC

22. Which of the following is not a transport layer function?

   A. Path determination

   B. End to end communication

   C. Flow control

   D. Reliability

23. Which of the following is not one of the protocols found at the TCP/IP application layer?

   A. UDP

   B. HTTP

   C. FTP

   D. SNMP

Routing Fundamentals and Subnets

The network layer interfaces to networks and provides the best end-to-end packet delivery services to its user, the transport layer. The network layer sends packets from the source network to the destination network.

Routers are devices that implement the network service. They provide interfaces for a wide range of links and subnetworks at various speeds. Routers are active and intelligent network nodes; therefore, they can participate in managing the network. Routers manage networks by providing dynamic control over resources and supporting the tasks and goals for networks: connectivity, reliable performance, management control, and flexibility.

In addition to the basic switching and routing functions, routers have implemented a variety of value-added features that help to improve the cost-effectiveness of the network. These features include sequencing traffic based on priority and traffic filtering.

Typically, routers are required to support multiprotocol stacks, each with its own routing protocols, and to allow these different environments to operate in parallel. In practice, routers also incorporate bridging functions and can serve as a limited form of hub.

IP addressing makes it possible for data that is passing over the network media of the Internet to find its destination. Because each IP address is a 32-bit value, there are four billion different IP address possibilities. IP addresses are hierarchical addresses, like phone numbers and zip codes. They provide a better way to organize computer addresses than MAC addresses, which are "one-dimensional" addresses (like social security numbers). IP addresses can be set in software, so they are flexible. MAC addresses are burned into hardware. Both addressing schemes are important for efficient communications among computers.

Concept Questions

Demonstrate your knowledge of these concepts by answering the following questions in the space provided.

1. Path determination occurs at the network layer. Routers are another type of internetworking device. These devices pass data packets among networks based on network protocol or layer 3 information. Explain how this process works.

   _____

   _____

2. Routers have the capability to make intelligent decisions as to the best path for delivery of data on the network. What criteria do routers use to make these decisions?

   _____

   _____

3. IP addresses are 32-bit values that are written as four octets separated with periods. To make them easier to remember, IP addresses are usually written in dotted notation with decimal numbers. IP addresses are used to identify a machine on a network and the network to which it is attached. What do dotted-decimal and hexadecimal mean?

   _____

   _____

   _____

   _____

4. Convert the following decimal numbers to hexadecimal numbers.

    A. 32,014

    B. 56,432

    C. 57,845

    D. 98,764

    E. 54,462

_____

_____

_____

_____

5. Convert the following hexadecimal numbers to decimal numbers.

    A. 23F6

    B. 6AB7

    C. 5FE3

    D. 87CE

    E. 59AC

_____

_____

_____

_____

6. Time-To-live (TTL) is a field that specifies the number of hops a packet may travel. Describe how this field can prevent a packet from looping endlessly.

_____

_____

7. Describe the process of encapsulation and de-encapsulation as a packet is switched from a router interface to another router interface.

_____

_____

8. List and describe four routing protocols.

_____

_____

9. List and describe four routed protocols.

_____

_____

Vocabulary Exercise

Define the following terms as completely as you can. Use the online curriculum or CCNA 1 Chapter 10 from the *Cisco Networking Academy Program CCNA 1 and 2 Companion Guide*, Revised Third Edition, for help.

address

broadcast address

broadcast storm

IP

ISPs

router

segment

subnet mask

subnetwork

Focus Questions

1. What type of addressing scheme does the network layer address use?

2. Switches can learn layer two addresses and routers can learn layer three addresses. Why must switches forward broadcasts, leading to possible broadcast storms?

3. What type of determination is the process the router uses to choose a course for the packet to travel to its destination?

_____

_____

4. At what layer does logical addressing occur?

_____

_____

5. When a computer is moved to a different network, what type of address remains the same and what type of address must be reassigned?

_____

_____

6. What is the difference between a flat addressing scheme and a hierarchical addressing scheme?

_____

_____

_____

_____

7. In the IP header, what information does the "total length" contain?

_____

_____

8. What three pieces of information does the subnet mask give to network devices?

_____

_____

9. What happens to a packet if there is no route found in the routing table for the packets destination network?

_____

_____

10. What are the two link-state routing protocols?

_____

_____

11. What are the benefits of subnetting?

_____

_____

CCNA Exam Review Questions

The following questions help you prepare for the CCNA Exam. Answers appear in Appendix B, "CCNA 1 and 2 Exam Review Questions Answer Key."

1. Which layer of the OSI model uses the Internet Protocol addressing scheme to determine the best way to move data from one place to another?

    A. Physical layer

    B. Data link layer

    C. Network layer

    D. Transport layer

2. Which of the following functions allows routers to evaluate available routes to a destination and to establish the preferred handling of a packet?

    A. Data linkage

    B. Path determination

    C. SDLC interface protocol

    D. Frame Relay

3. IP addresses are necessary for which of the following reasons?

    A. To identify a machine on a network and the network to which it is attached

    B. To identify a machine on a network

    C. To identify the network

    D. To keep track of who is on a network

4. Which of the following best describes a network address on the Internet?

    A. All four octets in the address are different.

    B. Each address is unique.

    C. The first three octets can be the same, but the last one must be different.

    D. Two of the four octets can be the same, but the other two must be different.

5. Who assigns the network portion of every IP address?

    A. The local network administrator

    B. The person who owns the computer

    C. The Network Information Center

    D. The host network administrator

6. The network number plays what part in an IP address?

    A. It specifies the network to which the host belongs.

    B. It specifies the identity of the computer on the network.

    C. It specifies which node on the subnetwork is being addressed.

    D. It specifies which networks the device can communicate with.

7. The host number plays what part in an IP address?

    A. It designates the identity of the computer on the network.

    B. It designates which node on the subnetwork is being addressed.

    C. It designates the network to which the host belongs.

    D. It designates which hosts the device can communicate with.

8. A Class A address is given to what sort of organization?

    A. An individual

    B. A medium-size company

    C. A large corporation

    D. A government

9. In a Class A address, which octets does InterNIC assign?

    A. The first octet

    B. The first and second octet

    C. The first, second, and third octets

    D. All the octets

10. In a Class A address, the value of the first octet can equal which of the following?

    A. 0 through 127

    B. 128 through 191

    C. 192 through 223

    D. 192 through 255

11. A Class B address is given to what sort of organization?

    A. An individual

    B. A medium-size company

    C. A large corporation

    D. A government

12. In a Class B address, which octets are assigned locally?

    A. The first octet

    B. The second octet

    C. The second and third octets

    D. The third and fourth octets

13. The address 129.21.89.76 is of which class?

    A. Class A

    B. Class B

    C. Class C

    D. Address not valid

14. Given a host with the IP address of 172.16.55.33 and the default subnet mask, what is the network number?

    A. 172.16.55.32

    B. 172.16.55.0

    C. 172.16.0.0

    D. 172.0.0.0

15. Which of the following addresses is a Class C address? (Choose all that apply.)

    A. 129.219.95.193

    B. 209.101.218.30

    C. 151.13.27.38

    D. 192.119.15.17

16. What address changes as a frame is received at each router?

    A. Layer 4 address

    B. Layer 3 address

    C. Layer 2 address

    D. All of the above

17. If you have only one class C network and you need to create 6 subnets with at least 22 hosts, on each subnet what will your subnet mask be?

    A. 255.255.255.0

    B. 255.255.255.128

    C. 255.255.255.192

    D. 255.255.255.224

18. If you have only one class C network and you need to create 11 subnets with at least 11 hosts, on each subnet what will your subnet mask be?

    A. 255.255.255.224

    B. 255.255.255.240

    C. 255.255.255.248

    D. 255.255.255.252

19. What is the maximum number of bits that can be borrowed from a Class C network?

    A. 2

    B. 4

    C. 6

    D. 8

20. What is the maximum number of bits that can be borrowed from a Class B network?

    A. 2

    B. 8

    C. 14

    D. 16

21. How many subnets are usable with a subnet mask of 255.255.252.0 with a Class B network?

    A. 62

    B. 64

    C. 256

    D. 1024

22. How many subnets are created with a subnet mask of 255.255.255.240 with a Class B network?

    A. 16

    B. 2048

    C. 4096

    D. 65,536

TCP/IP Transport and Application Layers

Services that are located in the transport layer enable users to segment several upper-layer applications onto the same transport layer data stream. These services also allow for the reassembly of the same upper-layer application segments at the receiving end.

The transport layer data stream provides transport services from the host to the destination. Services such as these are sometimes referred to as *end-to-end services*. The transport layer data stream is a logical connection between the endpoints of a network.

As the transport layer sends its data segments, it can also ensure the integrity of the data. One method of doing this is called *flow control* . Flow control avoids the problem of a host at one side of the connection overflowing the buffers in the host at the other side. Overflows can present serious problems because they can result in data loss.

Transport-layer services also allow users to request reliable data transport between hosts and destinations. To obtain such reliable transport of data, a connection-oriented relationship is used between the communicating end systems. Reliable transport can accomplish the following:

- It ensures that delivered segments will be acknowledged back to the sender.
- It provides for retransmission of any segments that are not acknowledged.
- It puts segments back into their correct sequence at the destination.
- It provides congestion avoidance and control.

The application layer supports the communicating component of an application. A computer application can require only information that resides on its computer. However, a network application might have a communicating component from one or more network applications.

Concept Questions

Demonstrate your knowledge of these concepts by answering the following questions in the space provided.

1. For data transfer to begin, both the sending and receiving application programs inform their respective operating systems that a connection will be initiated. How is this accomplished?

_____

_____

_____

_____

2. In concept, one machine places a call that the other must accept. If the receiving machine does not accept the call, what happens?

_____

_____

3. Protocol software modules in the two operating systems communicate by sending messages. Messages are sent across the network to verify that the transfer is authorized and that both sides are ready. How is this accomplished?

_____

_____

4. After all synchronization occurs, a connection is established and data transfer begins. How do both machines know that the data is flowing correctly?

_____

_____

5. Windowing is a process of flow control. Describe the operation of TCP window size?

_____

_____

6. The application layer provides services to application processes. What services are provided?

_____

_____

7. The application layer identifies and establishes the availability of intended communication partners and the resources that are required to connect with them. What are these resources?

_____

_____

8. The domain naming system was developed in order to associate the contents of a site with the address of that site. What is the intent of each major domain suffix?

_____

_____

9. Port numbers are used by FTP. What is the purpose of using both port 20 and port 21?

_____

_____

Vocabulary Exercise

Define the following terms as completely as you can. Use the online curriculum or CCNA 1 Chapter 11 from the *Cisco Networking Academy Program CCNA 1 and 2 Companion Guide*, Revised Third Edition, for help.

agent

_____

_____

application layer

_____

_____

best-effort delivery

_____

_____

client

client/server computing

DNS

domain server

flow control

FTP

full duplex

HTML

HTTP

IP address

NMS

redirector

SMTP

SNMP

TCP

_____

_____

Telnet

_____

_____

TFTP

_____

_____

transport layer

_____

_____

UDP

_____

_____

URL

_____

_____

window size

_____

_____

Focus Questions

1. What type of numbers is used to keep track of different conversations that cross the network at the same time?

_____

_____

2. What is the name of a protocol that combines connectionless and connection-oriented service?

_____

_____

3. What is the difference between TCP and UDP?

_____

_____

4. What is the field in a TCP segment that ensures correct sequencing of the arriving data?

_____

_____

5. Which protocols use UDP?

_____

_____

6. Which protocols use TCP?

_____

_____

7. What range of port numbers is reserved for public applications?

_____

_____

8. Which window type has a window size that is negotiated dynamically during the TCP session?

_____

_____

9. Which network application uses the direct interface that the application layer provides?

_____

_____

10. Which network application uses the indirect interface that the application layer provides?

_____

_____

11. Where is the server side of a client/server application located?

_____

_____

12. What is the looped routine that a client/server application constantly repeats?

_____

_____

13. What does DNS do?

_____

_____

14. Which two protocols do file utility programs use to copy and move files between remote sites?

_____

_____

15. Which protocol do remote-access programs use to directly connect to remote resources?

_____

_____

16. Describe the three key components of a SNMP network?

_____

_____

CCNA Exam Review Questions

The following questions help you prepare for the CCNA Exam. Answers appear in Appendix B, "CCNA 1 and 2 Exam Review Questions Answer Key."

1. Which of the following layers provides transport services from the host to the destination?

    A. Application

    B. Presentation

    C. Session

    D. Transport

2. Which of the following best describes the function of the transport layer?

    A. It establishes, manages, and terminates applications.

    B. It provides transport services from the host to the destination.

    C. It supports communication among programs such as electronic mail, file transfer, and web browsers.

    D. It translates between different data formats such as ASCII and EBCDIC.

3. Which of the following methods best describes flow control?

    A. A method to manage limited bandwidth

    B. A method of connecting two hosts synchronously

    C. A method to ensure data integrity

    D. A method to check data for viruses prior to transmission

4. Which of the following functions best describes flow control?

    A. It checks data packets for integrity and legitimacy prior to transmission.

    B. It avoids traffic backup by cycling hosts quickly through alternate send and receive modes during peak traffic periods.

    C. It connects two hosts over an exclusive high-speed link for critical data transfer.

    D. It avoids the problem of a host at one side of the connection, overflowing the buffers in the host at the other side.

5. Which of the following occurs in the transport layer when a connection is first established between computers in a network?

    A. Acknowledgment and retransmission

    B. Encapsulation and broadcasting

    C. Synchronization and acknowledgment

    D. Recovery and flow control

6. Which of the following occurs in the transport layer when data congestion occurs?

    A. Broadcasting

    B. Windowing

    C. Error recovery

    D. Flow control

7. Which of the following layers handles flow control and error recovery?

    A. Application

    B. Presentation

    C. Transport

    D. Network

8. Which of the following techniques allows multiple applications to share a transport connection?

    A. Broadcasting

    B. Synchronicity

    C. Encapsulation

    D. Segmentation

9. Which of the following best describes segmentation?

    A. It breaks data into smaller packets for faster transmission.

    B. It switches hosts from send to receive mode continuously during peak traffic periods.

    C. It allows multiple applications to share a transport connection.

    D. It transfers data from the presentation layer to the network layer for encoding and encapsulation.

10. Which of the following methods controls the amount of information transferred end-to-end and helps to enable TCP reliability?

    A. Broadcasting

    B. Windowing

    C. Error recovery

    D. Flow control

11. If the window size were set to 1, when would an acknowledgment of data packet receipt be sent back to the source?

    A. After one packet

    B. After two packets

    C. After three packets

    D. After four packets

12. If the window size were set to 3, when would an acknowledgment of data packet receipt be sent back to the source?

    A. After one packet

    B. After three packets

    C. After six packets

    D. After nine packets

13. Which of the following layers supports communication between programs, such as e-mail, file transfer, and web browsers?

    A. Application

    B. Presentation

    C. Session

    D. Transport

14. Which of the following is not a feature of UDP?

    A. Unreliable delivery of datagrams

    B. Connectionless service

    C. Connection oriented service

    D. Receives reliability for the upper layers of the OSI model

15. Which of the following is a network application?

    A. E-mail

    B. Word processor

    C. Web browser

    D. Spreadsheet

16. Which of the following is a computer application?

    A. Remote access

    B. File transfer

    C. Web browser

    D. E-mail

17. E-mail and file transfer are typical functions of which layer?

    A. Transport

    B. Network

    C. Application

    D. Presentation

18. What protocol is used to upgrade the IOS on a Cisco router?

    A. TFTP

    B. SMTP

    C. QOS

    D. PPP

CCNA 2: Routers and Routing Basics

WANs and Routers

One major characteristic of a wide-area network (WAN) is that the network operates beyond the local LAN's geographic scope. It uses the services of carriers, such as regional Bell operating companies (RBOCs), Sprint, and MCI.

WANs use serial connections of various types to access bandwidth over wide-area geographies. By definition, the WAN connects devices that are separated by wide areas. WAN devices include the following:

- Routers, which offer many services, including internetworking and WAN interface ports

- Switches, which connect to WAN bandwidth for voice, data, and video communication

- Modems, which interface voice-grade services and channel service units/digital service units

- Channel service units/data service units (CSUs/DSUs) that interface T1/E1 services and Terminal Adapters/Network Termination 1 (TA/NT1s)

- TA/NT1s that interface Integrated Services Digital Network (ISDN) services

- Communication servers, which concentrate on dial-in and dial-out user communication

Concept Questions

Demonstrate your knowledge of these concepts by answering the following questions in the space provided.

1. A WAN is used to interconnect local-area networks (LANs) that are typically separated by a large geographic area. A WAN operates at the OSI reference model physical and data link layers. The WAN provides for the exchange of data packets/frames between routers/bridges and the LANs that they support. Draw a WAN that includes three LANs.

2. Compare and contrast WANs and LANs layer by layer.

_____

_____

_____

_____

3. Routers and the modern PC have many hardware components in common. Which components are shared by a PC and a router?

_____

_____

_____

_____

4. There are many steps that must occur to communicate with a router using a PC. Explain both the hardware and software components needed to establish a terminal session with a Cisco router.

_____

_____

_____

_____

Vocabulary Exercise

Define the following terms as completely as you can. Refer to the online curriculum or CCNA 2 Chapter 1 from the *Cisco Networking Academy Program CCNA 1 and 2 Companion Guide*, Revised Third Edition, for help.

auxiliary port

_____

_____

console port

_____

_____

CSU

_____

_____

DCE

_____

_____

DSU

_____

_____

DTE

_____

_____

E1

_____

_____

Frame Relay

_____

_____

HDLC

_____

_____

ISDN

_____

_____

PPP

_____

_____

PTT

_____

_____

RBOC

_____

_____

T1

_____

_____

Focus Questions

1. Name and briefly describe four WAN devices.

    _____

    _____

2. Name two ways in which WANs differ from LANs.

    _____

    _____

3. What do the acronyms DTE and DCE stand for?

    _____

    _____

4. List three WAN physical layer standards.

    _____

    _____

5. List four WAN data link layer protocols.

    _____

    _____

6. List the two ports on a router that you can use to enter an initial configuration.

    _____

    _____

7. List the settings used in HyperTerminal to connect to the console port of a Cisco router.

_____

_____

8. What is the purpose of NVRAM on a Cisco router?

_____

_____

9. What is the purpose of RAM on a Cisco router?

_____

_____

10. What is the purpose of Flash on a Cisco router?

_____

_____

CCNA Exam Review Questions

The following questions help you review for the CCNA exam. Answers appear in Appendix B, "CCNA 1 and 2 Exam Review Questions Answer Key."

1. Which of the following best describes a WAN?

   A. It connects LANs that are separated by a large geographic area.

   B. It connects workstations, terminals, and other devices that are in a metropolitan area.

   C. It connects LANs that are within a large building.

   D. It connects workstations, terminals, and other devices that are within a building.

2. Which of the following are WAN technologies?

   A. Token Ring and ARCnet

   B. Frame Relay and ISDN

   C. Star and Banyan VINES

   D. CSU/DSU and ARCview

3. What service does a WAN provide to LANs?

   A. High-speed multiple access to data networks

   B. IP addressing and secure data transfer

   C. Exchange of data packets between routers and the LANs those routers support

   D. Direct routing with error checking

4. What type of connections do WANs use that LANs typically do not use?

 A. Parallel, lower speed

 B. Multiple, higher speed

 C. Multiple, lower speed

 D. Serial, lower speed

5. At which layers of the OSI model does a WAN operate?

 A. Physical and application

 B. Physical and data link

 C. Data link and network

 D. Data link and presentation

6. Which layers of the OSI model do WAN standards describe?

 A. Data link and network

 B. Data link and presentation

 C. Physical and application

 D. Physical and data link

7. How do WANs differ from LANs?

 A. WANs typically exist in defined geographic areas.

 B. WANs provide high-speed multiple access services.

 C. WANs use tokens to regulate network traffic.

 D. WANs use services of common carriers.

8. How are operational and functional connections for WANs obtained?

 A. From your local telephone company

 B. From InterNIC

 C. From RBOCs

 D. From the WWW Consortium (W3C)

9. What do the WAN physical layer standards describe?

 A. Interface between SDLC and HDLC

 B. How frames are sent and verified

 C. How voice and data traffic are routed

 D. Interface between DTE and DCE

10. Which of the following best describes what WAN data link protocols define?

    A. How frames are carried between systems on a single data link

    B. Methods for determining optimum path to a destination

    C. How data packets are transmitted between systems on multiple data links

    D. Methods for mapping IP addresses to MAC addresses

11. Which of the following is a WAN data link protocol?

    A. TCP/IP

    B. Point-to-Point Protocol

    C. EIGRP

    D. OSPF

12. Which of the following best describes data terminal equipment (DTE)?

    A. It is a physical connection between networks and users.

    B. It generates clocking signals to control network traffic.

    C. It is a device at the user end of a network.

    D. It is a physical device such as a modem and interface card.

13. Which of the following is an example of DTE?

    A. Interface card

    B. Modem

    C. Computer

    D. CSU/DSU

14. Which of the following best describes data circuit-terminating equipment (DCE)?

    A. It is a device at the user end of a network.

    B. It serves as the data source or destination.

    C. It is physical devices such as protocol translators and multiplexers.

    D. It is a physical connection between networks and users.

15. Which is an example of DCE?

    A. Multiplexer

    B. Modem

    C. Translator

    D. Computer

16. Which of the following best describes High-Level Data Link Control (HDLC)?

    A. It is a digital service that transmits voice and data over existing phone lines.

    B. It uses high-quality digital facilities and is the fastest WAN protocol.

    C. It provides router-to-router and host-to-network connections over synchronous and asynchronous circuits.

    D. It supports point-to-point and multipoint configurations and uses frame characters and checksums.

17. Which WAN protocol can be described as supporting point-to-point and multipoint configurations?

    A. HDLC

    B. Frame Relay

    C. PPP

    D. ISDN

18. Which WAN protocol can be described as using frame characters and checksums?

    A. ISDN

    B. Frame Relay

    C. PPP

    D. HDLC

19. Which of the following best describes Frame Relay?

    A. It uses high-quality digital facilities and is the fastest WAN protocol.

    B. It supports point-to-point and multipoint configurations, and it uses frame characters and checksums.

    C. It is a digital service that transmits voice and data over existing telephone lines.

    D. It provides router-to-router and host-to-network connections over synchronous and asynchronous circuits.

20. Which of the following are not used in a WAN?

    A. Hub

    B. Modem

    C. Router

    D. Communications server

21. Which WAN protocol can be described as the fastest WAN protocol?

    A. HDLC

    B. PPP

    C. Frame Relay

    D. ISDN

22. Which of the following best describes PPP?

    A. It uses high-quality digital facilities and is the fastest WAN protocol.

    B. It supports point-to-point and multipoint configurations, and it uses frame characters and checksums.

    C. It provides router-to-router and host-to-network connections over synchronous and asynchronous circuits.

    D. It is a digital service that transmits voice and data over existing telephone lines.

23. Which WAN protocol can be described as providing router-to-router and host-to-network connections over synchronous and asynchronous circuits?

    A. HDLC

    B. Frame Relay

    C. PPP

    D. ISDN

24. Which of the following best describes ISDN?

    A. It is a digital service that transmits voice and data over existing phone lines.

    B. It provides router-to-router and host-to-network connections over synchronous and asynchronous circuits.

    C. It uses high-quality digital facilities and is the fastest WAN protocol.

    D. It supports point-to-point and multipoint configurations, and it uses frame characters and checksums.

25. Which of the following is stored in NVRAM?

    A. The active Cisco IOS software image

    B. The backup configuration file for the router

    C. The backup Cisco IOS software image

    D. The active routing table

26. Which of the following cannot be accomplished using the console port?

    A. Troubleshoot problems

    B. Monitor the system

    C. Configure the router

    D. Capture data packets from a LAN

27. Where are console messages sent by default?

    A. All ports on the router

    B. Console Port

    C. Auxiliary Port

    D. Messages are sent to interface null 0 by default

28. What type of cable do you use to connect a PC to the console port?

    A. Patch cable

    B. Rollover

    C. Crossover

    D. EIA/TIA 568B

29. What type of cable do you use to connect a PC to a switch?

    A. Patch cable

    B. Rollover

    C. Crossover

    D. EIA/TIA 568B

30. What type of cable do you use to connect a switch to a hub?

    A. Patch cable

    B. Rollover

    C. Crossover

    D. EIA/TIA 568B

Introduction to Routers

The startup routines for Cisco IOS Software have the goal of starting router operations. The router uses information from the configuration file when it starts up. The configuration file contains commands to customize router operation. As you saw in Chapter 1, "WANs and Routers," if no configuration file is available, the system configuration dialog setup guides you through creating one. The router must deliver reliable performance connecting the user networks that it was configured to serve. To do this, the startup routines must do the following:

- Make sure that the router comes up with all its hardware tested.

- Find from memory and load the Cisco IOS Software image that the router uses for its operating system.

- Find from memory and apply the configuration statements about the router, including protocol functions and interface addresses.

The router makes sure that it comes up with tested hardware. When a Cisco router powers up, it performs a power-on self-test (POST). During this self-test, the router executes diagnostics from ROM on all modules. These diagnostics verify the basic operation of the CPU, memory, and network interface ports. After the router verifies the hardware functions, it proceeds with software initialization. You configure Cisco routers from the user interface that runs on the router console or terminal. You also can configure Cisco routers by using remote access. You must log in to the router before you can enter an EXEC command. For security purposes, the router has two levels of access to commands:

- **User mode**—Typical tasks include those that check the router status. In this mode, router configuration changes are not allowed.

- **Privileged mode**—Typical tasks include those that change the router configuration.

Concept Questions

Demonstrate your knowledge of these concepts by answering the following questions in the space provided.

1. Configuration files can come from the console, NVRAM, or a TFTP server. What are the different router modes?

   _____

   _____

2. What does it mean to configure a router?

   _____

   _____

   _____

   _____

3. Why must routers be configured?

_____

_____

4. The router initializes by loading a bootstrap, the operating system, and a configuration file. What does each of these items do?

_____

_____

_____

_____

5. If the router cannot find a configuration file, the router enters setup mode. What does the setup mode do?

_____

_____

_____

_____

6. The router stores a backup copy of the new configuration from setup mode. Where does the router store this backup copy?

_____

_____

7. One way you can make a router enter setup mode is to erase the startup configuration file and then reload the router. What are other ways you can make a router enter setup mode?

_____

_____

8. Prepare a flowchart of the startup (boot) sequence of a Cisco router.

9. A Cisco router has a fallback system to locate the operating system. What is the sequence that the router uses to locate and load the IOS?

_____

_____

10. A Cisco router has a fallback system to locate the configuration file. What is the sequence that the router uses to locate and load the configuration?

_____

_____

11. You can use the router to do the following: log in with the user password, enter privileged mode with the enable password, disable, or quit. What procedures would you follow to log in to the router?

_____

_____

12. You can use the following advanced help features: Command completion, command prompting, and syntax checking. Why would you need to use syntax checking?

_____

_____

13. Why is it important to have two different levels of command access?

_____

_____

14. Cisco router IOS has a naming convention to provide the network administrator details about the software. What are the major components of IOS naming?

_____

_____

15. There are two types of enable passwords. What are differences between these passwords?

_____

_____

Vocabulary Exercise

Define the following terms as completely as you can. Refer to the online curriculum or CCNA 2 Chapter 2 from the *Cisco Networking Academy Program CCNA 1 and 2 Companion Guide*, Revised Third Edition, for help.

configure terminal

_____

_____

CPU

_____

_____

DB 9 adapter

_____

_____

erase startup-config

_____

_____

NVRAM

_____

_____

privileged mode

_____

_____

reload

_____

_____

ROM monitor

_____

_____

user mode

_____

_____

Focus Questions

1. How do you access a router?

_____

_____

2. Distinguish between user mode and privileged mode.

_____

_____

3. What does it mean to configure a router? Why must routers be configured?

_____

_____

4. What do the prompts for user EXEC mode, privileged EXEC mode, and global configuration mode look like?

_____

_____

5. What are two basic tasks when first configuring a router?

_____

_____

6. In Cisco IOS Software, what is the user mode prompt and what is the privileged mode prompt?

_____

_____

7. What must you type at the user or privileged mode prompts to display a list of commonly used commands?

_____

_____

8. When in user mode, what must you do to enter privileged mode?

_____

_____

9. If you are unsure of the syntax or arguments for a command, what feature can be of great help to you?

_____

_____

10. What are the three main things the router accomplishes upon startup?

_____

_____

11. Briefly describe the router startup sequence.

_____

_____

_____

_____

_____

_____

12. What is the main purpose of setup mode?

_____

_____

13. During the system configuration dialog, you are prompted to set up "global parameters" and to set up "interfaces." Explain.

_____

_____

14. ROM monitor is used to recover from system failures and recover lost passwords. Describe how do you enter this mode and list the commands that are available.

_____

_____

15. After you have completed the setup command program and your configuration displays, you are asked whether you want to use this configuration. If you answer "yes," what happens?

_____

_____

CCNA Exam Review Questions

The following questions help you review for the CCNA exam. Answers appear in Appendix B, "CCNA 1 and 2 Exam Review Questions Answer Key."

1. What are the two modes of access to router commands for Cisco routers?

   A. User and privileged

   B. User and guest

   C. Privileged and guest

   D. Guest and anonymous

2. Why are there two modes of access to router commands on Cisco routers?

   A. One mode is for remotely working on the router, whereas the other mode is for directly working on the router via a console.

   B. One mode, which has many automatic sequences, is for new users, whereas the other mode is for experienced users who can issue direct commands.

   C. One mode lets a number of users see what's happening on the router, whereas the other mode lets a few users change how the router operates.

   D. One mode is for the initial router configuration and startup, whereas the other mode is for maintaining, updating, and changing the router after initial startup.

3. What can be done only in privileged mode on Cisco routers?

   A. Change the configuration.

   B. Enter commands.

   C. Check routing tables.

   D. Monitor performance.

4. How do you switch from user to privileged mode on Cisco routers?

   A. Type **admin** and enter a password.

   B. Type **root** and enter a password.

   C. Type **enable** and enter a password.

   D. Type **privileged** and enter a password.

5. What happens if you type **enable** on a Cisco router user interface?

   A. You switch to user mode.

   B. The last command entered is activated.

   C. A new LAN is added to the router table.

   D. You switch to privileged mode.

6. Which of the following commands is not available in the user access mode?

   A. **show**

   B. **ppp**

   C. **trace**

   D. **ping**

7. Which of the following is the user-mode prompt for Cisco router user interfaces?

   A. #

   B. >

   C. <

   D. |#

8. Which of the following is the privileged-mode prompt for Cisco router user interfaces?

   A. #

   B. >

   C. <

   D. |#

9. How do you log out of a Cisco router user interface?

   A. Press **Ctrl-Q**.

   B. Type **quit**.

   C. Type **exit**.

   D. Press **Ctrl-X**.

10. How can you get a list of commonly used commands from a Cisco router user interface?

   A. Type **list**.

   B. Press **Ctrl-C**.

   C. Press **Ctrl-?**.

   D. Type **?**.

11. What does the "More" prompt at the bottom of a screen on a Cisco router user interface mean?

   A. Multiple screens are available as output.

   B. Additional detail is available in the manual pages.

   C. Multiple entries are required in the command.

   D. Additional conditions must be stated.

12. How do you get to the next screen if "More" is indicated at the bottom of the current screen on a Cisco router user interface?

   A. Press the **Page Down** key.

   B. Press the **spacebar**.

   C. Press **End**.

   D. Press **Tab**.

13. Which keystroke(s) automatically repeat(s) the previous command entry on a Cisco router user interface?

   A. Left arrow

   B. Right arrow

   C. **Ctrl-R**

   D. **Ctrl-P**

14. What happens if you press **?** in a Cisco router user interface?

   A. You see all users logged in to the router.

   B. You list the last command you typed.

   C. You enter the help system.

   D. You find out which mode you are currently in.

15. What does it mean if you see the symbol ^ on a Cisco router user interface?

   A. There is an error in the command string.

   B. You are in Help mode.

   C. You must enter more information to complete the command.

   D. You are in privileged mode.

16. What would you type at the router user prompt if you wanted to see which **show** subcommands were available?

   A. **?**

   B. **command ?**

   C. **show ?**

   D. **list ?**

17. What would you type at the router user prompt if you wanted to see which configuration subcommands were available?

   A. **?**

   B. **command ?**

   C. **list ?**

   D. **config ?**

18. Which of the following commands is only available at the privileged access mode?

    A. **ping**

    B. **show**

    C. **trace**

    D. **ppp**

19. Which of the following is the correct order of steps in the Cisco router system startup routine?

    A. Locate and load the operating system, load the bootstrap, test the hardware, and locate and load the configuration file.

    B. Test the hardware, load the bootstrap, locate and load the operating system, and locate and load the configuration file.

    C. Load the bootstrap, locate and load the configuration file, test the hardware, and locate and load the operating system.

    D. Test the hardware, load the bootstrap, locate and load the configuration file, and locate and load the operating system.

20. Which of the following is *not* a step in the Cisco router system startup routine?

    A. Loading the bootstrap

    B. Power-up hardware self-test

    C. Enabling CDP on each interface

    D. Locating and loading the configuration file

21. Which of the following is an important function of POST?

    A. Determining the router hardware and software components and listing them on the console terminal

    B. Causing other instructions to be loaded into memory

    C. Executing diagnostics that verify the basic operation of router hardware

    D. Starting routing processes, supplying addresses for interfaces, and setting up media characteristics

22. Which of the following is an important result of Cisco IOS Software loading onto a router?

    A. Determining the router hardware and software components and listing them on the console terminal

    B. Causing other instructions to be loaded into memory

    C. Executing diagnostics that verify the basic operation of router hardware

    D. Starting routing processes, supplying addresses for interfaces, and setting up media characteristics

23. Which of the following is an important result of the configuration file loading onto a router?

    A. Determining the router hardware and software components and listing them on the console terminal

    B. Causing other instructions to be loaded into memory

    C. Executing diagnostics that verify the basic operation of router hardware

    D. Starting routing processes, supplying addresses for interfaces, and setting up media characteristics

24. Which of the following is *not* a function of the router system startup routine?

    A. Verifying the routing of protocol packets

    B. Testing of the basic operations of router hardware

    C. Causing other instructions to be loaded into memory

    D. Starting routing processes, supplying addresses for interfaces, and setting up media characteristics

25. When is the router setup mode executed?

    A. After the saved configuration file is loaded into the main memory

    B. When the network administrator needs to enter complex protocol features on the router

    C. When the router begins software initialization

    D. When the router cannot find a valid configuration file

26. Which of the following does *not* describe features of the router setup mode?

    A. Many default settings appear in square brackets.

    B. The prompt and command for the setup mode are "router# setup".

    C. The first line and title of the setup dialog is "System Configuration Dialog".

    D. Pressing the **Enter** key cancels dialog prompts.

27. Which of the following correctly describes a procedure for setup of router global and interface parameters on a router?

    A. A default parameter is shown in square brackets at every prompt.

    B. The router host name must be set.

    C. An enable secret password can be set, but it is not required.

    D. For each installed interface, a series of questions must be answered.

28. Which of the following does *not* correctly describe a procedure for setup of global and interface parameters on a router?

    A. An enable secret password must be entered.

    B. A default parameter is shown in square brackets at every prompt.

    C. Configuration values that you have determined for the installed interfaces are entered as parameters at the interface prompts.

    D. The router hostname must be set.

29. What information do you need to gather before starting a global or interface configuration session on a router?

    A. Brand and model of router and type of networks the router connects to directly

    B. Cisco IOS Software version and current register setting

    C. Which routing protocols will be needed, IP addresses of interface and subnets, and which interfaces are being used

    D. IP addresses of neighboring routers and size of Flash memory

30. Which of the following correctly describes the router setup script review?

    A. The **setup** command program displays the configuration that was created from your answers to the setup prompts.

    B. The **setup** command program asks you whether you want to change any of your answers.

    C. If you choose to use the displayed configuration, you select a location to save it to.

    D. If you choose not to use the configuration, you must reboot the router.

31. Which of the following correctly describes the procedure for modifying the script displayed upon completion of the router configuration process?

    A. The setup command program prompts you at each of the script lines as to whether you want to change your answers.

    B. When you choose not to accept the configuration, the router reboots.

    C. When you select the dialog lines that you want to change, the program prompts you again at those lines.

    D. The script tells you to use configuration mode to modify the configuration.

32. Which keystoke will take you to the end of the line?

    A. **Ctrl-A**

    B. **Ctrl-B**

    C. **Ctrl-E**

    D. **Ctrl-Z**

33. Which keystoke will allow you to exit configuration mode?

    A. **Ctrl-A**

    B. **Ctrl-B**

    C. **Ctrl-E**

    D. **Ctrl-Z**

34. Which of the following is not a Cisco IOS naming convention?

    A. Hardware platform

    B. Special features and capabilities

    C. Amount of RAM required

    D. Where the image runs

35. Which of the following is not listed by issuing the **show version** command?

    A. Hardware platform

    B. Configuration register setting

    C. Where the IOS was loaded

    D. How the router was restarted

    E. All of the above

Configuring a Router

Whether the router is accessed from the console or by a Telnet session through an auxiliary port, it can be placed in several modes. Each mode provides different functions:

- **User EXEC mode**—A "look-only" mode in which the user can view some information about the router but cannot change anything.

- **Privileged EXEC mode**—Supports the debugging and testing commands, detailed examination of the router, manipulation of configuration files, and access to configuration modes.

- **Setup mode**—Presents an interactive prompted dialog box at the console that helps the new user create a first-time, basic configuration.

- **Global configuration mode**—Implements powerful one-line commands that perform simple configuration tasks.

- **Other configuration modes**—Provide more complicated multiple-line configurations.

- **RXBOOT mode**—A maintenance mode that can be used, among other things, to recover lost passwords.

Concept Questions

Demonstrate your knowledge of these concepts by answering the following questions in the space provided.

1. The router is made up of configurable components. How are these components configured?

   _____

   _____

2. A router serial interface must be configured. What commands are needed to configure a router with a DCE cable attached?

   _____

   _____

3. A network administrator wants to encrypt passwords on a router. What does the command service password-encryption do?

   _____

   _____

4. Router interface descriptions are very useful during troubleshooting and network documentation. The interface description can contain the circuit identification, point of contact, phone number of point of contact, and what the interface connects to. Describe the process to add a description to an interface.

_____

_____

5. Explain the router password recovery procedure on 2600 and 2500 series routers.

Step-by-step procedure (2600 Router):

_____

_____

_____

_____

_____

_____

_____

_____

_____

_____

Step-by-step procedure (2500 Router):

_____

_____

_____

_____

_____

_____

_____

_____

_____

_____

_____

_____

6. The router has modes for examining, maintaining, and changing the components. What does the router do in examining mode?

_____

_____

7. When you issue the command **show interface serial 0** on an unconfigured router. What is the state of the interface?

_____

_____

Vocabulary Exercise

Define the following terms as completely as you can. Use the online curriculum or CCNA 2 Chapter 3 from the *Cisco Networking Academy Program CCNA 1 and 2 Companion Guide*, Revised Third Edition, for help.

CPU

_____

_____

DRAM

_____

_____

host table

_____

_____

NVRAM

_____

_____

RAM

_____

_____

TFTP

_____

_____

Focus Questions

1. Describe the procedure for setting the hostname on a Cisco router?

_____

_____

2. List three external configuration sources for Cisco routers.

_____

_____

3. The commands **copy running-config tftp** and **copy running-config startup-config** store the currently running configuration from RAM to _____ and _____, respectively.

4. List and describe the different router modes and interfaces that can be password protected.

_____

_____

5. List at least seven commands that can show router status and the configurable components about which they display information.

_____

_____

6. List the steps to completely erase all configuration information from a router.

_____

_____

CCNA Exam Review Questions

The following questions help you review for the CCNA exam. Answers appear in Appendix B, "CCNA 1 and 2 Exam Review Questions Answer Key."

1. Which of the following describes a location from which a router is configured?

   A. After a router is installed on the network, it can be configured from virtual terminals.

   B. Upon initial configuration, a router is configured from the virtual terminals.

   C. After a router is installed on the network, it can be configured via modem from the console terminal.

   D. Upon initial configuration, a router is configured via modem using the auxiliary port.

2. Which of the following does *not* describe external configuration of routers?

   A. Upon initial configuration, a router is configured from the console terminal.

   B. The router can be connected via modem using the console port.

   C. After a router is installed, it is configured from the console terminal.

   D. Configuration files can be downloaded from a TFTP server on the network.

3. Which of the following router components has these characteristics: stores routing tables, fast-switching cache, and packet hold queues?

   A. NVRAM

   B. RAM/DRAM

   C. Flash

   D. ROM

4. Which of the following router components has these characteristics: holds the operating system and microcode, retains its contents when you power down or restart, and allows software updates without replacing chips?

   A. NVRAM

   B. RAM/DRAM

   C. Flash

   D. ROM

5. Which of the following best describes the function of NVRAM?

    A. It provides temporary or running memory for the router's configuration file while the router is powered on.

    B. It stores the router's backup configuration file. The content is retained when you power down or restart.

    C. It holds the operating system image and microcode and enables you to update software without removing and replacing chips on the processor.

    D. It contains power-on diagnostics, a bootstrap program, and operating system software.

6. Which of the following does *not* describe a function of working storage RAM in a router?

    A. A bootstrap program performs tests and then loads the Cisco IOS software into memory.

    B. A saved version of the configuration file is accessed from NVRAM and loaded into main memory when the router initializes.

    C. The EXEC part of the IOS software handles packet buffering and the queuing of packets.

    D. The operating system image is usually executed from the main RAM and loaded from an input source.

7. Which of the following is the router mode that supports debugging and testing commands, manipulation of configuration files, and detailed examination of the router?

    A. Global configuration mode

    B. RXBOOT mode

    C. Privileged EXEC mode

    D. Setup mode

8. Which of the following describes functions of the user EXEC mode of a router?

    A. It presents an interactive prompted dialog that helps the new user create a first-time basic configuration.

    B. It implements powerful one-line commands that perform simple configuration tasks.

    C. It is used for recovery from catastrophe, such as to retrieve lost passwords.

    D. It allows the user to view some information about the router but not change anything.

9. If you are in global configuration mode, what does the router prompt look like?

    A. router #

    B. router (config) #

    C. router-config #

    D. r-config #

10. When you are in user mode, what does the router prompt look like?

    A. router -

    B. router >

    C. router #

    D. router

11. What is the command you enter to gain access to privileged EXEC mode?

    A. **ena**

    B. **p exec**

    C. **exec**

    D. **enable p-exec**

12. Which of the following does *not* correctly describe the function of a router status command?

    A. **show version**—Displays configuration of the system hardware, the names and sources of configuration files, and the boot images.

    B. **show mem**—Displays statistics about the router's memory, including Memory-free pool statistics.

    C. **show buffers**—Displays statistics for the buffer pools on the router.

    D. **show interfaces**—Displays statistics for all interfaces that are configured on the router.

13. If you type **show ?** at the router > prompt, what appears on the screen?

    A. Nothing; this is not a valid command.

    B. All the items that can be shown in user mode.

    C. The status of the router.

    D. Information about the version of the IOS that is currently running.

14. Which of the following describes a function of the **show running-config** Cisco IOS Software command?

    A. It enables an administrator to see the image size and startup configuration commands that the router will use on the next restart.

    B. It displays a message at the top showing how much nonvolatile memory has been used.

    C. It enables an administrator to see the configuration of the processes and interrupt routines.

    D. It enables an administrator to see the current running configuration on the router.

15. Which of the following describes a function of the **show startup-config** Cisco IOS Software command?

    A. It enables an administrator to see the current running configuration on the router.

    B. It displays a message at the top showing how much nonvolatile memory has been used.

    C. It enables an administrator to see the reason for the last system reboot.

    D. It displays this message at the top: Current Configuration.

16. The **show interface serial** Cisco IOS Software router command can display which one of the following lines of information?

    A. IOS 4500 Software (C4500-J-M), Experimental Version 11.2.

    B. DECNET routing is enabled.

    C. Serial1 is up, line protocol is up.

    D. System image file is c4500-j-mz.

17. The **show version** Cisco IOS Software router command can display which one of the following lines of information?

    A. IOS 4500 Software (C4500-J-M), Experimental Version 11.2.

    B. Hardware is MK5025.

    C. Internet Protocol routing is enabled.

    D. Internet address is 183.8.64.129.

18. The **show protocols** Cisco IOS Software router command can display which one of the following lines of information?

    A. Serial1 is up, line protocol is up.

    B. Compiled Fri 28-Jun-96.

    C. AppleTalk routing is enabled.

    D. ROM; System Bootstrap, Version 5.1(1).

19. What kind of information *cannot* be obtained when you enter **show interface** in the user mode?

    A. The MAC address for all interfaces

    B. The IP address for all interfaces

    C. The number of users who are logged in to each interface

    D. The encapsulation protocol for each interface

20. If you type **show interface E0** at the prompt router#, which of the following best shows what the first lines of the response would look like if the interface were up?

    A.
```
Ethernet0 is up, line protocol is up
Address is 0000.0f92.c54b (bia 0000.0f92.c54b)
Internet address is 223.8.151.1/24
MTU 1500 bytes, BW 10000 Kbit, DLY 1000 usec, rely 255/255,
load 1/255
Encapsulation ARPA, loopback not set, keepalive set (10sec)
```

    B.
```
Ethernet0 is up, line protocol is up
Hardware is Lance, address is 0000.0f92.c54b (bia 0000.0f92.c54b)
Internet address is 223.8.151.1/24
ARP type: ARPA, ARP Timeout 05:00:00
Encapsulation ARPA, loopback not set, keepalive set (10sec)
```

    C.
```
Ethernet0 is up, line protocol is up
Hardware is Lance, address is 0000.0f92.c54b (bia 0000.0f92.c54b)
Internet address is 223.8.151.1/24
MTU 1500 bytes, BW 10000 Kbit, DLY 1000 usec, rely 255/255, load  1/255
Encapsulation ARPA, loopback not set, keepalive set (10sec)
```

    D.
```
Ethernet0 is up, line protocol is up
Address is 0000.0f92.c54b (bia 0000.0f92.c54b)
Internet address is 223.8.151.1/24
Subnet Mask is 255.255.255.255/24
Encapsulation ARPA, loopback not set, keepalive set (10sec)
```

21. Why might you want to issue **show startup-config** and **show running-config** commands?

    A. It is time to update the Cisco IOS Software image and you need to kill certain router processes before proceeding.

    B. You want to determine the time since the router booted and the current register setting.

    C. The router suddenly isn't working right and you want to compare the initial state to the present state.

    D. You want to find out where the Cisco IOS Software image booted from and which version is being used.

22. Why should the enable password be different from the enable secret password?

    A. The router asks that the passwords be changed monthly if they are the same.

    B. It provides an additional category of users.

    C. The enable password can be read directly from the configuration file.

    D. Cisco IOS Software behaves badly if the passwords are the same.

23. What file(s) would you find in NVRAM?

    A. Cisco IOS Software and configuration files

    B. Configuration file

    C. Backup copy of Cisco IOS Software

    D. Limited version Cisco IOS Software and Registry files

24. Which of the following is *not* a function of the privileged EXEC configure command?

    A. Configuring a router from a virtual terminal

    B. Configuring a TFTP server from a virtual terminal

    C. Configuring a router from the console terminal

    D. Loading a configuration from a network TFTP server

25. Which of the following is *not* a step in using the **copy running-config tftp** command to store the current router configuration? (The steps are listed in order.)

    A. Enter the **copy running-config tftp** command.

    B. Enter the IP address of the router.

    C. Enter the name you want to assign to the configuration file.

    D. Confirm your choices.

26. Which of the following is *not* a step in using the **copy tftp running-config** command to load a router configuration file that is stored on a TFTP server? (The steps are listed in order.)

    A. Enter the **copy tftp running-config** command.

    B. Select either a host configuration file or a network configuration file.

    C. Enter the IP address of the remote host from which you retrieve the configuration file.

    D. Enter the name of the server to which you will load the file.

27. Which of the following does *not* correctly describe using a TFTP server to maintain router configuration files?

    A. A host configuration file contains commands that apply to all routers and terminal servers on the network.

    B. The convention for all filenames is UNIX-based.

    C. The default filename is hostname-config for the host file.

    D. Reconfiguration of the router occurs as soon as a new file is downloaded to the router.

28. You want to replace your current configuration file with one that is located on a TFTP server. What is the process you need to go through to do this?

    A. router (config)# **copy tftp running-config**
    Host or network configuration file [host]?
    IP address of remote host [255.255.255.255]? 131.108.6.155
    Name of configuration file [Router-config]? paris.3
    Configure using paris.3 from 131.108.6.155 [confirm] y
    Booting paris.3 from 131.108.6.155: !! [OK – 874/16000 bytes]
    Router (config)#

    B. router # **copy tftp running-config**
    Host or network configuration file [host]?
    IP address of remote host [255.255.255.255]? 131.108.6.155
    Configure using paris.3 from 131.108.6.155 [confirm] y
    Booting paris.3 from 131.108.6.155: !! [OK – 874/16000 bytes]
    Router#

    C. router # **copy tftp running-config**
    Host or network configuration file [host]?
    Name of configuration file [Router-config]? paris.3
    Configure using paris.3 from 131.108.6.155 [confirm] y
    Booting paris.3 from 131.108.6.155: !! [OK – 874/16000 bytes]
    Router#

    D. router # **copy tftp running-config**
    Host or network configuration file [host]?
    IP address of remote host [255.255.255.255]? 131.108.6.155
    Name of configuration file [Router-config]? paris.3
    Configure using paris.3 from 131.108.6.155 [confirm] y
    Booting paris.3 from 131.108.6.155: !! [OK – 874/16000 bytes]
    Router#

29. What is the function of the **configure memory** router command?

    A. It loads configuration information from NVRAM.

    B. It erases the contents of NVRAM.

    C. It stores in NVRAM the current configuration that is in RAM.

    D. It displays the configuration that is saved in NVRAM.

30. What is the function of the **copy running-config startup-config** router command?

    A. It loads configuration information from NVRAM.

    B. It erases the contents of NVRAM.

    C. It stores in NVRAM the current configuration that is in RAM.

    D. It displays the configuration that is saved in NVRAM.

31. You added a new LAN onto your network; therefore, you updated your routing table and other parts of your configuration file. What command do you need to issue to save the new configuration file?

    A. **copy config startup-config**

    B. **copy running-config startup-config**

    C. **configure memory**

    D. **copy startup-config config-running**

32. Which router mode is a subset of the EXEC commands that are available at the privileged EXEC mode?

    A. Global configuration mode

    B. User EXEC mode

    C. Interface configuration mode

    D. Router configuration mode

33. What is the system prompt for the user EXEC router mode?

    A. Router>

    B. Router#

    C. Router(config)#

    D. User EXEC

34. What happens when you type **exit** at a router mode prompt?

    A. A configuration mode prompt appears.

    B. The router logs you off.

    C. The router backs out one mode level.

    D. A question prompt appears, requesting a network device location.

35. What does the router prompt look like when you are in global configuration mode?

    A. Router#

    B. Router (config-router)#

    C. Router (config)#

    D. Router-config#

36. If you want to back completely out of configuration mode, what must you enter?

    A. **exit**

    B. **no config-mode**

    C. **Ctrl-E**

    D. **Ctrl-Z**

37. If you press **Ctrl-Z** to get out of configuration mode, where do you end up?

    A. User EXEC mode

    B. Privileged EXEC mode

    C. Global configuration mode

    D. Router mode

38. If you are planning to configure an interface, what prompt should be on the router?

    A. Router (config)#

    B. Router (config-in)#

    C. Router (config-intf)#

    D. Router (Config-if)#

39. Which of the following does *not* describe a procedure for using the router global configuration mode?

    A. You type **configure** to enter global configuration mode.

    B. You can specify the terminal, NVRAM, or a file on a server as the source of configuration commands.

    C. You can type commands to configure specific interfaces.

    D. You can type a command to reach a prompt for the interface configuration mode.

40. Which of the following is the system prompt for the global configuration mode?

    A. Router#

    B. Router(config)#

    C. Router(config-global)#

    D. Router(config-router)#

41. Which of the following does *not* describe a step in the procedure for using the router configuration mode?

    A. Enter a global router protocol command type at the global configuration prompt.

    B. The Router(config-router)# prompt indicates that you are in router configuration mode.

    C. Defaults can be selected for all available command options.

    D. Finish using this mode with the command **exit**.

42. Which of the following does *not* describe a step in the procedure for using the interface configuration mode?

    A. Enter a global interface type and number command at the global configuration prompt.

    B. The Router(config-if)# prompt indicates that you are in interface configuration mode.

    C. Interfaces can be turned on and off by using commands in this mode.

    D. Interface types are enabled at subcommands in this mode.

43. Which of the following is the correct order for the process of configuring a router? (Assume that you have already made router changes in configuration mode.)

    A. Save the changes to backup, decide whether the changes are your intended results, examine the results, and examine the backup file.

    B. Examine the results, decide whether the changes are your intended results, save the changes to backup, and examine the backup file.

    C. Decide whether the changes are your intended results, examine the backup file, save the changes to backup, and examine the results.

    D. Examine the results, save the changes to backup, decide whether the changes are your intended results, and examine the backup file.

44. Which of the following best describes the process of configuring a router?

    A. Examine the results, make the changes in configuration mode, remove the changes, and decide whether the changes are your intended results.

    B. Decide whether the changes are your intended results, make changes in the configuration mode, examine the results, and remove the changes.

    C. Make the changes in configuration mode, decide whether the changes are your intended results, examine the results, and remove the changes.

    D. Make the changes in configuration mode, examine the results, decide whether the changes are your intended results, and remove the changes.

45. Which of the following commands can you use to save router configuration changes to a backup?

    A. Router# **copy running-config tftp**

    B. Router# **show running-config**

    C. Router# **config mem**

    D. Router# **copy tftp running-config**

46. Which of the following is *not* a command to remove router configuration changes?

    A. Router(config)# **no ...**

    B. Router# **config mem**

    C. Router# **copy running-config startup-config**

    D. Router# **copy tftp running-config**

47. Which of the following correctly describes password configuration on routers?

    A. All passwords are established in the privileged EXEC mode.

    B. All passwords alter the password character string.

    C. A password can be established on all incoming Telnet sessions.

    D. The **enable** password command restricts access to user EXEC mode.

48. Which of the following does *not* describe password configuration on routers?

    A. Passwords can be established in every configuration mode.

    B. A password can be established on any console terminal.

    C. The enable secret password uses an encryption process to alter the password character string.

    D. All password establishment begins in the global configuration mode.

49. When you are setting passwords for vty 0 4, for what access point to the router are you setting a password for?

    A. Line consoles

    B. Telnet sessions

    C. Remote host router

    D. Virtual hosts

50. The password that is set up with the **enable-secret** command is to control direct access to what?

    A. User EXEC mode

    B. Configure Interface mode

    C. Privileged EXEC mode

    D. Global configuration mode

51. Which of the following correctly describes procedures for confirming router identification?

    A. Routers should be named only after initial testing of the network.

    B. If no name is configured, the system automatically assigns the router a number.

    C. You name the router in global configuration mode.

    D. The login banner can be configured to display system error messages.

52. Which of the following does *not* describe procedures for confirming router identification?

    A. If no name is configured, the system default router name is Router.

    B. Naming your router to be the host should be one of the first network configuration tasks.

    C. The login banner is configured in global configuration mode.

    D. You can configure a message-of-the-day banner to display on specified terminals.

53. You want to create a message to let people know a little something about the network when they log in. What command enables you to do this?

   A. **banner mesg**

   B. **banner motd**

   C. **daily mesg**

   D. **daily motd**

54. What is the function of the **erase startup-config** command?

   A. It deletes the backup configuration file in NVRAM.

   B. It deletes the bootstrap image from Flash memory.

   C. It deletes the current Cisco IOS Software image from NVRAM.

   D. It deletes the current running configuration from Flash memory.

55. What is the function of the **reload** command?

   A. It loads a backup configuration file from a TFTP server.

   B. It saves the new Cisco IOS Software image to Flash memory.

   C. It reboots the router.

   D. It loads the new configuration file in NVRAM.

56. Which router command deletes the backup configuration file in NVRAM?

   A. **delete backup-config**

   B. **erase backup-config**

   C. **delete startup-config**

   D. **erase startup-config**

57. Which router command causes the router to reboot?

   A. **reload**

   B. **restart**

   C. **reboot**

   D. **rerun**

58. What are the major elements of a typical router configuration?

   A. Passwords, interfaces, routing protocols, DNS

   B. Boot sequence, interfaces, tftp server, NVRAM

   C. NVRAM, ROM, DRAM, interfaces

   D. Interfaces, routing protocols, configuration register, flash

59. In a password recovery procedure, immediately after issuing a **Ctrl-Break** upon router startup, what should the configuration register setting be?

    A. 0x2102

    B. 0x2142

    C. 0x0000

    D. 0x10F

60. In a password recovery procedure, just before saving the running configuration and after you enable a new secret password, what should the configuration register setting be?

    A. 0x2102

    B. 0x2142

    C. 0x0000

    D. 0x10F

Learning About Other Devices

Cisco Discovery Protocol (CDP) is a layer 2 protocol that connects lower physical media and upper network layer protocols. CDP is used to obtain information about neighboring devices. This information shows the types of devices that are connected, the router interfaces they are connected to, the interfaces that are used to make the connections, and the model numbers of the devices. CDP is media and protocol independent, and it runs on all Cisco equipment as well as on the Subnetwork Access Protocol.

Concept Questions

Demonstrate your knowledge of these concepts by answering the following questions in the space that is provided.

1. The command **show cdp neighbors** displays layer 2 information about directly connected devices. List and describe the information obtained with CDP.

   _____

   _____

2. Test network connectivity layer by layer. Testing commands include ping, trace, and debug. What is the difference between trace and ping?

   _____

   _____

3. Cisco Discovery Protocol operates a layer 2 of the OSI model. How is CDP useful in troubleshooting layer three problems?

   _____

   _____

4. The **cdp run** command is used to enable CDP on the entire router. Why might a network administrator turn off CDP on a networking device?

   _____

   _____

5. The command **cdp enble** is used to enable CDP on an interface. Why might a network administrator turn off CDP on an interface?

_____

_____

6. Telnet is used to test layer seven of the OSI model. Telnet is used to log in and issue commands to a remote router. Why would a network administrator want to suspend and then resume a Telnet session to a router?

_____

_____

Vocabulary Exercise

Define the following terms as completely as you can. Use the online curriculum or CCNA 2 Chapter 4 from the *Cisco Networking Academy Program CCNA 1 and 2 Companion Guide*, Revised Third Edition, for help.

CDP

_____

_____

CDP enable

_____

_____

CDP run

_____

_____

CDP timers

_____

_____

interface

_____

_____

Ping

_____

_____

resume

_____

_____

Telnet

_____

_____

trace

_____

_____

Focus Questions

1. Briefly describe what the **show cdp neighbors** command can tell you about a network.

_____

_____

2. Briefly describe the three major routed protocols that CDP provides information.

_____

_____

3. Using the OSI model and the commands **telnet**, **ping**, **trace**, **show ip route**, and **show interface**, describe the basic testing of a network.

_____

_____

4. Briefly describe what the **show cdp** command can tell you about a router

_____

_____

5. Briefly describe the function of the **cdp timers** command.

_____

_____

6. Briefly describe the difference between the **resume** command or pressing the **Enter** key during a suspended Telnet session.

_____

_____

7. Briefly why Telnet is an excellent network-troubleshooting tool.

_____

_____

CCNA Exam Review Questions

The following questions help you review for the CCNA exam. Answers appear in Appendix B, "CCNA 1 and 2 Exam Review Questions Answer Key."

1. Which one of the following is a function of CDP?

A. It provides a way to use an echo to evaluate the path-to-host reliability.

B. It provides a way to determine whether a routing table entry exists.

C. It provides a way to see the current running configuration on the local router.

D. It provides a way to access summaries of configurations on directly connected devices.

2. Which of the following is a characteristic of CDP?

    A. It runs over OSI Layer 3.

    B. It allows CDP devices that support different network layer protocols to learn about each other.

    C. It obtains information about neighboring devices only if the administrator enters commands.

    D. It obtains information only about devices that are running TCP/IP.

3. What steps does the network administrator have to take to make CDP run at system startup?

    A. Type **cdp enable** at the first router prompt.

    B. Type **cdp enable** at the first privilege EXEC router prompt.

    C. CDP runs automatically at startup.

    D. Type **cdp enable** at any prompt and then save the config file.

4. Which of the following is a function of the **show cdp** command?

    A. It displays information about any CDP-enabled router on the network.

    B. It displays information on a console that is connected to any node in the network.

    C. It helps evaluate delays over network paths and path-to-host reliability.

    D. It identifies neighboring routers' host names and IP addresses.

5. Which of the following is *not* provided by the CDP **show** command to tell about neighbor routers?

    A. Processes list, with information about the active processes

    B. Port identifier, such as Ethernet0, Serial1, and so forth

    C. The device's hardware platform

    D. Address list, with addresses for supported protocols

6. Which of the following is a function of the **cdp enable** command?

    A. It boots up the Cisco IOS software and implements diagnostic testing.

    B. It displays values of the CDP timers.

    C. It begins CDP's dynamic discovery function on the router's interfaces.

    D. It discards expired hold-time values.

7. Which of the following is *not* a function of the **show cdp interface** command?

    A. It displays the values of the CDP timers.

    B. It displays the reasons for system reboot.

    C. It displays the interface status.

    D. It displays the encapsulation that CDP uses.

8. Which of the following is a function of the **show cdp entry** [*device_name*] command?

    A. It establishes a connection to a remote router.

    B. It displays the cached CDP entry for every directly connected CDP router.

    C. It enables an administrator to see the IP addresses of the targeted router.

    D. It displays version information about the network protocols that are running on the router.

9. Which of the following is *not* a function of the **show cdp entry** [*device_name*] command?

    A. It displays the cached CDP entry for every directly connected CDP router.

    B. It displays all Layer 3 addresses that are present on the router.

    C. It displays how long ago the CDP frame arrived from the router.

    D. It displays version information about the router.

10. Which of the following is a function of the **show cdp neighbors** command?

    A. It displays the device capability code of remote routers.

    B. It displays the path-to-host reliability of a network connection.

    C. It displays the encapsulation of the protocols that neighbor routers use.

    D. It displays the neighbor's remote port type and number.

11. Which of the following is *not* a function of the **show cdp neighbors** command?

    A. It displays the cached CDP entry for every directly connected CDP router.

    B. It displays the CDP updates that are received on any network router.

    C. It displays information like that from **show cdp entry** when **show cdp neighbors detail** is used.

    D. It displays neighbor device IDs.

12. Why would you use the **show cdp neighbors** command?

    A. To get a snapshot view of the routers in the network

    B. To get an overview of the routers that are directly connected to you

    C. To get the IP addresses for neighboring routers

    D. To build a routing table for all routers that are in the network neighborhood

13. Which of the following is a feature of Telnet router operations?

    A. Telnet is typically used to connect a router to neighbor routers.

    B. A router can have only one incoming Telnet session at a time.

    C. A Telnet session can be suspended and then resumed.

    D. To initiate a Telnet session, you must know the name of the host.

14. Which of the following layer 3 protocols does CDP not provide information?

    A. Appletalk

    B. IP

    C. IPX

    D. SNMP

15. Which of the following is a feature of CDP

    A. Obtains information about only directly connected Cisco devices

    B. Runs on all Cisco equipment

    C. Operates at layer two of the OSI model.

    D. Media and protocol dependent

16. Which of the following is not a feature of Ping

    A. Used to test the application layer of the OSI model

    B. Uses echo and echo reply

    C. Verifies reachability

    D. Very basic testing tool

17. What is the default log out time for a Telnet session to a router?

    A. 300 seconds

    B. 600 seconds

    C. 900 seconds

    D. Never

18. What is the key sequence to suspend a Telnet session?

    A. **Ctrl-B**

    B. **Ctrl-Shift**

    C. **Ctrl-Shift-6**, then x

    D. **Ctrl-Alt-Shift-Delete**

Managing Cisco IOS Software

The default source for Cisco IOS Software depends on the hardware platform; most commonly, though, the router looks to the configuration commands that are saved in NVRAM. Cisco IOS Software offers several alternatives. You can specify other sources where the router should look for software or the router uses its own fallback sequence as necessary to load software.

Settings in the configuration register enable alternatives for where the router will bootstrap Cisco IOS Software. You can specify enabled configuration-mode boot system commands to enter fallback sources for the router to use in sequence. Save these statements in NVRAM to use during the next startup with the command **copy running-config startup-config**. The router uses these commands as needed, in sequence, when it restarts. If NVRAM lacks boot system commands that the router can use, the system has its own fallback alternatives. The router falls back and uses the default Cisco IOS Software image in Flash memory. If Flash memory is empty, the router tries its next TFTP alternative. The router uses the configuration register value to form a filename from which to boot a default system image that is stored on a network server.

Cisco develops many versions of IOS. The IOS supports different types of hardware and features. To identify the different versions of IOS Cisco developed a naming convention. The main fields in the naming convention are

- Hardware Platform
- Feature Set
- File Format
- Version Number

Concept Questions

Demonstrate your knowledge of these concepts by answering the following questions in the space that is provided.

Routers boot Cisco IOS Software from

- Flash
- TFTP server
- ROM (not full Cisco IOS)
- Multiple source options that provide flexibility and fallback alternatives

  1. Explain the process by which a router locates Cisco IOS software.

  _____

  _____

  2. Explain the configuration register.

  _____

  _____

3. Boot system commands may be added to the startup configuration to allow a fallback sequence in loading the IOS. What is the purpose of having different versions of IOS as a fallback?

_____

_____

4. If the configuration register is set for 0x2101 the boot system commands in the startup configuration file will not be used. Explain why?

_____

_____

5. Compare and contrast the boot options for obtaining Cisco IOS Software from Flash memory, from the network, and from ROM.

_____

_____

_____

_____

_____

_____

6. Describe the course of action the router will take if the Cisco IOS in flash is corrupted.

_____

_____

7. Describe the **show version** command and all the information it tells you.

_____

_____

8. Describe the processes for creating a software image backup, upgrading the image from a network, and loading a software image backup.

_____

_____

_____

_____

_____

9. If the router is booted into ROM monitor, what commands are available?

_____

_____

10. List and describe the four parts of the Cisco IOS naming convention.

_____

_____

_____

11. List and describe the four parts the Cisco IOS file name c2600-js-l_121-3.bin.

_____

_____

_____

_____

Vocabulary Exercise

Define the following terms as completely as you can. Refer to the online curriculum or CCNA 2 Chapter 5 from the _Cisco Networking Academy Program CCNA 1 and 2 Companion Guide_, Revised Third Edition, for help.

boot field

_____

_____

boot system

_____

_____

checksum

_____

_____

configuration register

_____

_____

copy command

_____

_____

copy flash tftp

_____

_____

copy run tftp

_____

_____

copy run start

_____

_____

copy start tftp

_____

_____

copy tftp flash

_____

_____

copy tftp start

_____

_____

copy tftp run

_____

_____

EEPROM

_____

_____

feature set

_____

_____

file format

_____

_____

flash

_____

_____

hardware platform

_____

_____

NVRAM

_____

_____

Ping

_____

_____

ROM

_____

_____

ROM monitor

_____

_____

TFTP Server

_____

_____

UDP

_____

_____

version number

_____

_____

xmodem

_____

_____

Focus Questions

1. Why might there be different versions of router operating systems?

_____

_____

_____

2. Where can routers boot Cisco IOS Software from?

    A. Flash memory

    B. A TFTP server

    C. Both A and B

3. The router cannot be configured to look elsewhere if Cisco IOS Software is not in Flash memory.

    A. True

    B. False

4. The configuration register is an n-bit register in NVRAM. What is the value of n?

    A. 8

    B. 16

    C. 32

5. What command would you use to check the configuration register setting?

    A. **configure terminal**

    B. **config-register**

    C. **show version**

6. What does the first E in EEPROM stand for?

    A. Erasable

    B. Electronically

    C. Enable

7. Which component is not required by a router to operate correctly?

    A. A configuration file

    B. A valid Cisco IOS image

    C. A DNS server

CCNA Exam Review Questions

The following questions help you review for the CCNA exam. Answers appear in Appendix B, "CCNA 1 and 2 Exam Review Questions Answer Key."

1. Which of the following correctly describes a method for specifying how a router loads Cisco IOS Software?

   A. Designate fallback sources for the router to use in sequence from NVRAM.

   B. Configure the Cisco IOS Software image for the location where it will bootstrap.

   C. Manually boot a default system image at a virtual terminal.

   D. Manually boot a default system image at the network server.

2. Which of the following is the sequence that the router uses for automatic fallback to locate Cisco IOS Software?

   A. Flash, NVRAM, TFTP server

   B. NVRAM, TFTP server, Flash

   C. NVRAM, Flash, TFTP server

   D. TFTP server, Flash, NVRAM

3. Which of the following does *not* describe configuration register settings for Cisco IOS Software bootstrapping?

   A. The order in which the router looks for system bootstrap information depends on the boot field setting.

   B. You change the configuration register setting with the command **config-register**.

   C. Use a hexadecimal number when setting the configuration register boot field.

   D. Use the **show running-config** command to check the boot field setting.

4. Which of the following information does the Cisco IOS Software **show version** command display?

   A. Statistics about the router's memory

   B. Name of the system image

   C. Information about the Flash memory device

   D. Status of configured network protocols

5. Which of the following commands is used to discover the configuration register setting?

   A. **show register**

   B. **show running-config**

   C. **show version**

   D. **show startup-config**

6. Which of the following does *not* correctly describe a fallback option for booting Cisco IOS Software?

   A. Flash memory provides storage that is not vulnerable to network failures.

   B. Loading Cisco IOS Software from a TFTP server is a good option if Flash memory becomes corrupted.

   C. The system image that is booted from ROM is usually a complete copy of Cisco IOS Software.

   D. ROM might contain an older version of Cisco IOS Software.

7. Which of the following correctly describes preparing to use a TFTP server to copy software to Flash memory?

    A. The TFTP server must be another router or a host system such as a UNIX workstation or a laptop computer.

    B. The TFTP host must be a system that is connected to an Ethernet network.

    C. The name of the router that contains the Flash memory must be identified.

    D. The Flash memory must be enabled.

8. Which of the following is *not* a step in preparing to copy software from a TFTP host to Flash memory?

    A. Check the router to make sure you can see and write into Flash.

    B. Verify that the router has sufficient room to accommodate Cisco IOS Software.

    C. Use the **show ip route** command to make sure you can access the TFTP server over the TCP/IP network.

    D. Check the TFTP server to make sure you know the file or file space for the Cisco IOS Software image.

9. Which of the following does *not* describe the procedure to verify sufficient room in Flash memory for copying software?

    A. Use the **show flash** command.

    B. Identify the total memory in Flash, which is the available memory.

    C. Compare the available memory with the length of the Cisco IOS Software image to be copied.

    D. If there is not enough available memory, you can try to obtain a smaller Cisco IOS Software image.

10. How would you determine the size of the Cisco IOS Software image file on a TFTP server?

    A. Go to the Cisco website and consult the image file size table.

    B. Type **show version** on your router.

    C. Type **dir** or **ls** on the TFTP server.

    D. Telnet to the TFTP server and issue a **show files** command.

11. Which of the following is the fastest way to make sure the TFTP server is reachable prior to trying to transfer a Cisco IOS Software image file?

    A. Trace the TFTP server.

    B. Ping the TFTP server.

    C. Telnet to the TFTP server.

    D. Call the TFTP server administrator.

12. Why do you need to determine the file size of the Cisco IOS Software image on the TFTP server before transferring it to your router?

    A. To check that there is enough space in Flash to store the file.

    B. To verify that the file is the correct Cisco IOS Software for your router.

    C. To complete a trivial File Transfer Protocol (FTP) operation, the file size must be known.

    D. To calculate the download time for the file and the amount of time that the router will be out of service.

13. What information is *not* provided in the Cisco IOS Software image filename system?

    A. Capabilities of the image

    B. Platform on which the image runs

    C. Where the image runs

    D. Size of the image

14. Which of the following is *not* part of the procedure for creating a Cisco IOS Software image backup to a TFTP server?

    A. Use the **show flash** command to learn the name of the system image file.

    B. Enter the **copy flash tftp** command to begin the copy process.

    C. Enter the IP address of the router that is holding the image file.

    D. Rename the file during transfer.

15. Why does an administrator create a Cisco IOS Software image backup?

    A. To verify that the copy in Flash is the same as the copy in ROM

    B. To provide a fallback copy of the current image prior to copying the image to a new router

    C. To create a fallback copy of the current image as part of procedures during recovery from system failure

    D. To create a fallback copy of the current image prior to updating with a new version

16. Which of the following is *not* part of the procedure for loading a new Cisco IOS Software image to Flash memory from a TFTP server? (The procedures are listed in correct order.)

    A. Back up a copy of the current software image to the TFTP server.

    B. Enter the **copy flash tftp** command to download the new image from the server.

    C. The procedure asks if you are willing to erase Flash.

    D. A series of Vs on the display indicates successful check run verification.

17. Which of the following is *not* part of the procedure for loading a backup Cisco IOS Software image to Flash memory from a TFTP server? (The procedures are listed in correct order.)

    A. Enter the **copy tftp flash** command.

    B. A prompt asks you for the IP address of the TFTP server.

    C. If a file with the same name exists in Flash memory, the file that is being copied automatically replaces it.

    D. Enter the **reload** command to boot up the router using the newly copied image.

18. What is the initial boot attempt if the router register is set to Ox2100?

    A. ROM monitor

    B. TFTP server

    C. ROM

    D. Flash

19. What is the initial boot attempt if the router register is set to Ox2101?

    A. ROM monitor

    B. TFTP server

    C. ROM

    D. Flash

20. What is the initial boot attempt if the router register is set to Ox2102?

    A. ROM monitor

    B. TFTP server

    C. ROM

    D. Flash

21. Which one of the following commands will boot a router while in ROM monitor mode?

    A. rommon22>**config-register 0x2102**

    B. rommon2>**boot flash**

    C. rommon5>**boot flash:ios image name**

    D. rommon17>**boot system flash: ios image name**

22. Which of the following is not a part of the Cisco IOS naming convention?

    A. Hardware Platform

    B. Feature Set

    C. Version Number

    D. Flash size

23. Which hardware platform is supported by the image named c2600-d-l-120-5.bin?

    A. 1205

    B. 2500

    C. 2600

    D. 1720

24. What feature set is supported by the image named c2600-d-l-120-5.bin?

    A. IP only

    B. Desktop

    C. Binary

    D. IP/IPX

Routing and Routing Protocols

Which path should traffic take through the cloud of networks? Path determination occurs at Layer 3 of the OSI reference model, which is the network layer. The path determination function enables a router to evaluate the available paths to a destination and to establish the preferred handling of a packet.

Routing services use network topology information when evaluating network paths. This information can be configured by the network administrator or collected through dynamic processes that are running in the network.

The network layer interfaces to networks and provides best-effort, end-to-end packet delivery services to its user, the transport layer. The network layer sends packets from the source network to the destination network based on the IP routing table.

After the router determines which path to use, it proceeds with forwarding the packet. The router takes the packet it accepted on one interface and forwards it to another interface or port that reflects the best path to the packet's destination.

Concept Questions

Demonstrate your knowledge of these concepts by answering the following questions in the space that is provided.

1. Internetworking functions of the network layer include network addressing and best-path selection for traffic. What is best-path selection?

   _____

   _____

2. In network addressing, one part of the address is used to identify the path that the router uses and the other is used for ports or devices on the network. Which part of the address is used to identify the path that the router uses?

   _____

   _____

3. Routed protocols allow routers to direct user traffic, and routing protocols work between routers to maintain path tables. Explain this key difference.

   _____

   _____

4. Network discovery for distance-vector routing involves exchange of routing tables. Problems can include slow convergence. What other problems can occur as a result of exchanging routing tables?

_____

_____

5. The distance vector routing protocol RIP has a metric and update timers. What is the metric and what are the default update timer settings?

_____

_____

6. The distance vector routing protocol IGRP has metrics and update timers. What are the IGRP metrics and default update timer settings?

_____

_____

7. For link-state routing, routers calculate the shortest paths to other routers. Problems can include inconsistent updates. What other problems might occur with link-state routing?

_____

_____

8. A link-state routing protocol can provide for faster convergence over a distance vector routing protocol. What are some other advantages of using a link-state routing protocol over a distance vector routing protocol?

_____

_____

_____

_____

9. Balanced hybrid routing uses attributes of both link-state and distance-vector routing and can apply paths to several protocols. What advantages does balance hybrid routing offer?

_____

_____

_____

_____

Vocabulary Exercise

Define the following terms as completely as you can. Refer to the online curriculum or CCNA 2 Chapter 6 from the *Cisco Networking Academy Program CCNA 1 and 2 Companion Guide*, Revised Third Edition, for help.

administrative distance

_____

_____

convergence

_____

_____

default route

_____

_____

delay

_____

_____

dynamic routing

_____

_____

EIGRP

_____

_____

header

_____

_____

hop

_____

_____

hop count

_____

_____

IGRP

_____

_____

OSPF

_____

_____

RIP

_____

_____

routing metric

_____

_____

routing protocol

_____

_____

static route

_____

_____

stub network

_____

_____

Focus Questions

1. What is the purpose of a routing protocol?

_____

_____

2. Distinguish between routed protocols and routing protocols.

_____

_____

_____

_____

3. Describe the process to add the directly connected networks 192.5.5.0 and 172.16.0.0 to be advertised by RIP?

_____

_____

4. List and briefly describe at least five examples of routing metrics.

_____

_____

_____

_____

5. Briefly describe distance-vector routing.

_____

_____

6. Briefly describe how a router learns about routes to a network.

_____

_____

7. Briefly describe how to configure a static route.

_____

_____

CCNA Exam Review Questions

The following questions help you review for the CCNA exam. Answers appear in Appendix B, "CCNA 1 and 2 Exam Review Questions Answer Key."

1. What function allows routers to evaluate available routes to a destination and to establish the preferred handling of a packet?

    A. Data linkage

    B. Path determination

    C. SDLC interface protocol

    D. Frame Relay

2. What information do routing services use to evaluate network paths?

   A. MAC addresses

   B. Name server tables

   C. Network topology

   D. ARP requests

3. Where can routing services obtain the network topology information that is needed to evaluate network paths?

   A. From RARP and ARP tables

   B. From network name servers

   C. From bridges talking to routers during messaging sessions

   D. From information that dynamic processes collect

4. What two functions does a router use to relay packets from one data link to another?

   A. Link-state testing and convergence

   B. Convergence and switching

   C. Path determination and link-state testing

   D. Path determination and switching

5. How does the network layer send packets from the source to the destination?

   A. It uses an IP routing table.

   B. It uses ARP responses.

   C. It refers to a name server.

   D. It refers to the bridge.

6. What happens at the router during a switching operation?

   A. The router changes from link-state to distance-vector mode.

   B. A packet that is accepted on one interface is forwarded to another interface or port that reflects the best path to the destination.

   C. A test message is sent over the proposed route to make sure it is operational.

   D. The received packet has the header stripped, read, and a new header attached listing the next stop on the route.

7. Which one of the following has the lowest administrative distance?

   A. A static route with an IP address as the next hop

   B. IGRP

   C. RIP

   D. A static route with an interface as the next hop

8. How does the network layer avoid unnecessary broadcast messages?

   A. By using error-trapping algorithms

   B. By using consistent end-to-end addressing

   C. By using name servers to do lookup functions

   D. By using link-state detection

9. Which one of the following is not a factor that should be considered when implementing a routing protocol?

   A. Bandwidth requirements.

   B. Processing requirements

   C. Router memory requirements

   D. Router location

10. What two parts of an address do routers use to forward traffic through a network?

    A. Network address and host address

    B. Network address and MAC address

    C. Host address and MAC address

    D. MAC address and subnet mask

11. Which term below means all routers have the same or consistent routing knowledge of the network?

    A. Converged

    B. Balanced

    C. Congruent

    D. Concave

12. How does a router make path selections?

    A. By looking at the network portion of the address

    B. By looking at the host portion of the address

    C. By looking at mean distances between routers

    D. By looking at the port or device on the network

13. What does the host address specify?

    A. Type of device

    B. Distance to the nearest network hub

    C. Specific port or device on the network

    D. Network the device is on

14. How does the host portion of an address help a router in its path determination function?

    A. It defines a path through the network.

    B. It contains distance information that can be used to calculate the shortest route.

    C. It refers to a specific port on the router that leads to an adjacent router in that direction.

    D. It tells the router the type of device and its distance from the router.

15. What does the switching function of a router do?

    A. It allows greater throughput and capacity by multitasking.

    B. It allows the router to accept a packet on one interface and forward it on another interface.

    C. It exchanges the old header of a data packet for a new header that includes path information for the next router.

    D. It changes the router from receive and send mode to broadcast mode when part of the network fails.

16. Which of the following best describes a routed protocol?

    A. It provides enough information to allow a packet to be forwarded from host to host.

    B. It provides information that is necessary to pass data packets up to the next highest network layer.

    C. It allows routers to communicate with other routers to maintain and update address tables.

    D. It allows routers to bind MAC and IP addresses together.

17. Which of the following is an example of a routed protocol?

    A. RIP

    B. IP

    C. IGRP

    D. OSPF

18. Which of the following best describes a routed protocol?

    A. It passes data packets to the next highest network layer.

    B. It binds MAC and IP addresses together.

    C. It defines the format and use of fields within a packet.

    D. It exchanges routing tables and shares routing information between routers.

19. Which of the following best describes a routing protocol?

    A. It provides information to allow a packet to be forwarded from host to host.

    B. It binds MAC and IP addresses together.

    C. It defines the format and use of fields within a data packet.

    D. It allows routers to communicate with other routers to maintain and update address tables.

20. Which of the following best describes the difference between routed versus routing protocols?

    A. Routed protocols are used between routers to maintain tables, whereas routing protocols are used between routers to direct traffic.

    B. Routed protocols use distance-vector algorithms, whereas routing protocols use link-state algorithms.

    C. Routed protocols are used between routers to direct traffic, whereas routing protocols are used between routers to maintain tables.

    D. Routed protocols use dynamic addressing, whereas routing protocols use static addressing.

21. What happens when a data-link frame is received on a router interface?

    A. The packet header is removed and a new one with additional routing information is attached.

    B. A frame header is sent to check the path integrity prior to sending the packet on toward its destination.

    C. The packet is sent to the nearest bridge, which forwards it to the next router or the final destination.

    D. The header is examined to determine the destination network and consults the routing table to see which outgoing interface is associated with that network.

22. What happens after a router has matched the destination network with an outgoing interface?

    A. The packet is sent to the nearest bridge that forwards it to the next router or the final destination.

    B. A frame header is sent to check the path integrity prior to sending the packet on toward its destination.

    C. The packet is queued for delivery to the next hop in the path.

    D. The packet header is removed and a new one with additional routing information is attached.

23. Which of the following static routes has the lowest administrative distance?

    A. Router(config)#**ip route 10.10.10.0 255.255.255.0 172.16.5.1 200**

    B. Router(config)#**ip route 10.10.10.0 255.255.255.0 172.16.5.1**

    C. Router(config)#**ip route 10.10.10.0 255.255.255.0 s0**

    D. Router(config)#**ip route 10.10.10.0 255.255.255.0 172.16.5.1 101**

24. What is the control information called that is placed in front of data in a data packet?

    A. Addressing

    B. Header

    C. Trailer

    D. Encapsulate

25. Which of the following best describes a hop?

    A. Passage of a data packet between two routers

    B. Device that connects two or more networks

    C. Shortest distance between source and destination

    D. Exchange and copying of ARP tables between two noncontiguous network devices

26. What is the passage of a data packet between two routers called?

    A. Exchange

    B. Hop

    C. Transmittal

    D. Signaling

27. Which of the following best describes multiprotocol routing?

    A. Capability to send packets simultaneously out different ports

    B. Capability to shift from static to dynamic routing as network loads change

    C. Capability to maintain routing tables for several routed protocols concurrently

    D. Capability to rewrite frame headers to formats that are compatible with different networks

28. What does multiprotocol routing allow routers to do?

    A. Rewrite frame headers to formats that are compatible with different networks

    B. Shift from static to dynamic routing as network loads change

    C. Send packets simultaneously out different ports

    D. Deliver packets from several routed protocols over the same data links

29. Which of the following best describes static routing?

    A. A route that the network administrator manually enters into a routing table

    B. A route that is received from the local name server

    C. A route that is automatically entered into a routing table

    D. An optimum route between devices as determined by the RARP table

30. Which of the following best describes dynamic routing?

    A. Automatic updating of routing tables whenever new information is received from the internetwork

    B. Manual entry of data into a routing table by the network administrator

    C. Following preset paths from device to device

    D. RARP server determining optimum route between devices and copying those routes into a routing table

31. What type of routing occurs without the intervention of a network administrator?

    A. Default

    B. Dynamic

    C. Progressive

    D. Static

32. What is one advantage of static routing?

    A. It is more secure because parts of an internetwork can be hidden.

    B. It requires little active management by the network administrator.

    C. It adjusts automatically to topology or traffic changes.

    D. It can compensate for router failures by using alternate paths.

33. What is one advantage of using static routing on a stub network?

    A. It compensates for route failures by using alternative paths.

    B. It requires little active management by the network administrator.

    C. It adjusts automatically to topology or traffic changes.

    D. It avoids the network overhead required by dynamic routing.

34. What are the two major classes of routing algorithms?

    A. Checksum and link state

    B. Checksum and traffic load

    C. Distance vector and traffic load

    D. Distance vector and link state

35. Which of the following best describes a distance vector protocol?

    A. It determines the direction and distance to any link in the internetwork.

    B. Each router maintains a complex database of internetwork topology information.

    C. Computationally, it is rather complex.

    D. Its method of routing prevents loops and minimizes counting to infinity.

36. What do distance vector algorithms require of routers?

    A. Default routes for major internetwork nodes in case of corrupted routing tables

    B. Sending its entire routing table in each update to its neighbors

    C. Fast response times and ample memory

    D. Maintaining a complex database of internetwork topology information

37. Why is it important in distance vector algorithms for routers to send copies of their routing table to neighboring routers?

    A. To prevent error propagation

    B. To stop routing loops

    C. To enable split horizon mapping

    D. To communicate topology changes quickly

38. What is a major drawback of distance vector algorithms?

   A. More network traffic

   B. Computationally difficult

   C. Prone to routing loops

   D. Cannot implement hold-down timers

39. What is one disadvantage of distance vector algorithms?

   A. Routers do not know the exact topology of an internetwork, only distances between points.

   B. They have more network traffic.

   C. Computationally, they are difficult.

   D. They cannot implement hold-down timers.

40. What is one advantage of distance vector algorithms?

   A. They are not likely to count to infinity.

   B. They implement easily on large networks.

   C. They are not prone to routing loops.

   D. They are simpler computationally.

41. Which of the following best describes link-state algorithms?

   A. They recreate the exact topology of the entire internetwork.

   B. They require minimal computations.

   C. They determine distance and direction to any link on the internetwork.

   D. They use little network overhead and reduce overall traffic.

42. Which of the following best describes link-state algorithms?

   A. They use little network overhead and reduce overall traffic.

   B. Each router broadcasts information about the network to all nodes on the network.

   C. They determine distance and direction to any link on the internetwork.

   D. They use little network overhead and increase overall traffic.

43. Which of the following is true about link-state routing algorithms?

   A. They require less network traffic than distance-vector algorithms.

   B. Computationally, they are rather simple.

   C. They require less router memory and slower response times.

   D. They maintain full knowledge of distant routers and how they interconnect.

44. Which of the following best describes convergence?

    A. When messages simultaneously reach a router and a collision occurs

    B. When several routers simultaneously route packets along the same path

    C. When all routers in an internetwork have the same knowledge of the structure and topology of the internetwork

    D. When several messages are being sent to the same destination

45. Which of the following terms describes an internetwork state in which all routers have the same knowledge of the structure and topology of the internetwork?

    A. Congruence

    B. Equivalence

    C. Correspondence

    D. Convergence

46. Why is fast convergence a desirable attribute of a routing protocol?

    A. It reduces the time period over which routers make incorrect routing decisions.

    B. It reduces network traffic.

    C. It reduces routing loop time.

    D. It reduces memory requirements of local routers.

47. After a network topology change, which of the following routing protocol characteristics reduces incorrect or wasteful routing decisions?

    A. Symmetry

    B. Convergence

    C. Equivalence

    D. Correspondence

48. What is a routing loop?

    A. A route to often-requested destinations

    B. A network path that is circular and has no branches

    C. A packet that cycles repeatedly through a constant series of network nodes

    D. A process that routers go through when performing self diagnostics

49. What is the process called in which packets never reach their destination but instead cycle repeatedly through the same series of network nodes?

    A. Split horizon

    B. End-to-end messaging

    C. Convergence

    D. Routing loop

50. Why do routing loops occur?

    A. There is slow convergence after a modification to the internetwork.

    B. Split horizons are artificially created.

    C. Network segments fail catastrophically and take other network segments down in a cascade effect.

    D. The network administrator never established or initiated default routes.

51. Why do routing loops occur?

    A. Split horizons are artificially created.

    B. A network device fails, and that information is slowly passed to all the routers in the internetwork.

    C. The network administrator never established or initiated default routes.

    D. Network segments fail catastrophically and take other network segments down in a cascade effect.

52. Why does the problem of counting to infinity occur?

    A. Split horizon

    B. Noncongruence

    C. Slow convergence

    D. Router inequivalence

53. Which of the following best describes the count to infinity problem?

    A. Routers continuously increment the hop count as a routing loop proceeds.

    B. Packets cycle repeatedly through a constant series of network nodes.

    C. During heavy traffic periods, freak collisions can occur and damage the packet headers.

    D. After a split horizon occurs, two sets of metrics exist for the same destination, and neither matches that in the routing table.

54. How can the count to infinity problem be prevented?

    A. By forcing a routing loop

    B. By invoking a split horizon process

    C. By tracking network traffic levels and regulating flow

    D. By imposing an arbitrary hop-count limit

55. How can the count to infinity problem be solved?

    A. By initiating a routing loop

    B. By defining infinity as some maximum number

    C. By switching from distance-vector to link-state mode

    D. By forcing a router convergence and reconciliation

56. What happens when the hop count exceeds the maximum in a routing loop?

    A. The loop ends and the data packet is returned to the source for retransmission later.

    B. The default route is recalled and used.

    C. The network is considered unreachable, and the loop ends.

    D. A count to infinity is initiated, and a split horizon is invoked.

57. How can the count to infinity problem be prevented?

    A. By using routing loops

    B. By using split horizon routing systems

    C. By increasing router memory

    D. By using hold-down timers

58. Which of the following best describes hold-down timers?

    A. Timer that synchronizes the router table update process

    B. Time during which messages are held if network segment is temporarily unavailable

    C. Time that is allowed before intervention to halt routing loop

    D. Time during which routers will neither send nor receive updated routing tables

59. Why are hold-down timers useful?

    A. They flush bad information about a route from all routers in the network.

    B. They force all routers in a segment to synchronize switching operations.

    C. They reduce the amount of network traffic during high traffic periods.

    D. They provide a mechanism for bypassing failed sections of the network.

60. When are routers placed in a hold-down state?

    A. When a routing loop occurs

    B. When a link in a route fails

    C. When a routing table becomes corrupted

    D. When convergence occurs too slowly

61. How does a hold-down timer work?

    A. By holding messages in routing loops for a given time period, the hold-down timer reduces network traffic at peak times.

    B. When the hop count exceeds a fixed value, the hold-down timer holds the message until a split horizon is established.

    C. When a router receives an update indicating that a network is inaccessible, the router marks the route and starts a hold-down timer.

    D. When a count is started, a hold-down timer is started, too; if the count continues after a given time period, the timer halts the process and returns control to the nearest router.

62. What are the major two link-state concerns?

   A. Split horizons and convergence

   B. Processing and memory requirements

   C. Routing loops and equivalence

   D. Table copying and counting to infinity

63. Which of the following best describes link-state advertisement (LSA)?

   A. Broadcast message that occurs in response to a convergence call

   B. Broadcast message that relays state of data links (up or down) to all routers

   C. Broadcast packet that contains information about neighbors and path costs

   D. Broadcast packet that is initiated by an active routing loop

64. What are LSAs used for?

   A. To halt routing loops

   B. To determine path metrics

   C. To broadcast convergence calls

   D. To maintain routing tables of receiving routers

65. What is the most complex and important aspect of link-state routing?

   A. Making sure all routers get all the necessary LSA packets

   B. Ensuring that convergence occurs rapidly

   C. Avoiding routing loops during initial startup

   D. Providing mechanisms for split horizons and count to infinity avoidance

66. What happens if routers have different sets of LSAs?

   A. A checksum procedure is initiated and faulty routing tables are repaired.

   B. Routes become unreachable because routers disagree about a link.

   C. A master comparison is forced, and subsequent convergence on a single routing table occurs.

   D. A broadcast message is sent with the master copy of the routing table to all routers.

67. What is one problem with link-state updating?

   A. It is easy to start a routing loop and subsequent count to infinity.

   B. Routers can become unreachable because they do not have a complete picture of the internetwork.

   C. In synchronizing large networks, it is difficult to tell which updates are correct.

   D. If the master routing table is corrupted, the entire network will go down.

68. What is one problem with link-state updating?

    A. Routers can become unreachable because they don't have a complete picture of the internetwork.

    B. It is easy to start a routing loop and subsequent count to infinity.

    C. If the master routing table is corrupted, the entire network will go down.

    D. The order of router startup alters the topology that was learned.

69. Which of the following is correct?

    A. Distance-vector routing gets all topological data from the routing tables of its neighbors, whereas link-state routing develops a map of the network by accumulating LSAs.

    B. Distance-vector routing develops a map of the network, whereas link-state routing gets topological data from the routing tables of its neighbors.

    C. Distance-vector routing requires a lot of bandwidth and network overhead, whereas link-state routing requires considerably less.

    D. Distance-vector routing has a quick convergence time, whereas link-state routing has a slow convergence time and is prone to routing loops.

70. Which of the following is correct?

    A. Distance-vector routing requires a lot of bandwidth and network overhead, whereas link-state routing requires considerably less.

    B. Distance-vector routing determines the best path by adding to the metric value it receives, whereas link-state routing has the routers calculating their own shortest path to destinations.

    C. Distance-vector routing has quick convergence time, whereas link-state routing has a slow convergence time and is prone to routing loops.

    D. Distance-vector routing has the routers calculate their own shortest path to destinations, whereas link-state routing determines the best path by adding to the metric value it receives from its neighbors.

71. Which of the following is correct?

    A. Distance-vector routing has a quick convergence time, whereas link-state routing has a slow convergence time and is prone to routing loops.

    B. Distance-vector routing requires a lot of bandwidth and network overhead, whereas link-state routing requires considerably less.

    C. Distance-vector routing updates for topology change with periodic table updates, whereas link-state routing updates are triggered by topology changes.

    D. Distance-vector routing updates are triggered by topology changes, whereas link-state routing updates for topology change with periodic scheduled table updates.

72. Which of the following best describes hybrid routing?

    A. It uses distance vectors to determine best paths, but topology changes trigger routing table updates.

    B. It uses distance-vector routing to determine best paths between topology during high-traffic periods.

    C. It uses topology to determine best paths but does frequent routing table updates.

    D. It uses topology to determine best paths but uses distance vectors to circumvent inactive network links.

Distance Vector Routing Protocols

As you know, routers can be configured to use one or more IP routing protocols. In this chapter, you learn the initial configuration of the router to enable the Routing Information Protocol (RIP) and the Interior Gateway Routing Protocol (IGRP). In addition, you learn how to monitor IP routing protocols.

After the router tests the hardware and loads the Cisco IOS system image, it finds and applies the configuration statements. These entries provide the router with details about router-specific attributes, protocol functions, and interface addresses. Remember that if the router cannot locate a valid startup-config file, it enters an initial router configuration mode called setup mode or system configuration dialog.

With the setup mode command facility, you can answer questions in the system configuration dialog. This facility prompts you for basic configuration information. The answers that you enter allow the router to build a sufficient but minimal router configuration that includes the following:

- An inventory of interfaces
- An opportunity to enter global parameters
- An opportunity to enter interface parameters
- A setup script review
- An opportunity to indicate whether or not you want the router to use this configuration

After you confirm setup mode entries, the router uses the entries as a running configuration. The router also stores the configuration in NVRAM as a new startup-config, and you can start using the router. For additional protocol and interface changes, you can use the enable mode and enter the command **configure**.

Concept Questions

Demonstrate your knowledge of these concepts by answering the following questions in the space that is provided.

1. Routers can be configured to use one or more IP routing protocols. Identify and briefly explain the different IP routing protocols.

   _____

   _____

2. RIP and IGRP are two IP routing protocols. Compare and contrast these two IP routing protocols.

   _____

   _____

3. RIP uses route poisoning for loop prevention by marking a network that goes down with a hop count of 16. List and describe other loop prevention mechanisms that RIP uses to prevent loops

_____

_____

Vocabulary Exercise

Define the following terms as completely as you can. Refer to the online curriculum or CCNA 2 Chapter 7 from the *Cisco Networking Academy Program CCNA 1 and 2 Companion Guide*, Revised Third Edition, for help.

adjacent neighbor

_____

_____

autonomous system

_____

_____

bandwidth

_____

_____

convergence

_____

_____

count to infinity

_____

_____

delay

_____

_____

distance vector routing algorithm

_____

_____

dynamic routing

_____

_____

hold-down timer

_____

_____

IGRP

_____

_____

link-state routing algorithm

_____

_____

MTU

_____

_____

poison reverse

_____

_____

reliability

_____

_____

RIP

_____

_____

routing metric

_____

_____

routing protocol

_____

_____

routing table

_____

_____

routing update

_____

_____

split horizon

_____

_____

static route

_____

_____

triggered update

_____

_____

Focus Questions

1. The system administrator manually defines default routes as the route to take when no route to the destination is known. Default routes are also known as which of the following?

   A. Dynamic routes

   B. Default subnet

   C. Default network

2. Default routes are configured by using the _____ command, while in the _____ prompt.

   A. **ip default route**; Router (config)#

   B. **ip default-network**; Router (config)#

   C. **ip default-route**; Router(config-if)#

3. Which of the following is used to communicate within a given autonomous system?

   A. Routing Information Protocols

   B. Exterior Routing Protocols

   C. Interior Routing Protocols

4. Routing protocols can be configured on a router while in which of the following modes?

   A. Router#

   B. Router(config)#

   C. Router(config-if)#

5. Which of the following protocols sends updated routing table information onto the network every 90 seconds?

   A. IGRP

   B. RIP

   C. Exterior Gateway Protocol (EGP)

6. What kind of entries does a router initially refer to?

   A. Entries about networks or subnets that are directly connected

   B. Entries that it has learned about from the Cisco IOS software

   C. Entries whose IP address and mask information are known

   D. Entries that it has learned about from other routers

7. Which of the following best describes a static route?

   A. A routing table entry that is used to direct frames for which a next hop is not explicitly listed in the routing table

   B. A route that is explicitly configured and entered into the routing table and that takes precedence over routes that dynamic routing protocols choose

   C. A route that adjusts automatically to network topology or traffic changes

   D. A route that adjusts involuntarily to direct frames within a network topology

8. Which of the following best describes a default route?

    A. A routing table entry that directs frames for which a next hop is not explicitly listed in the routing table

    B. A route that is explicitly configured and entered into the routing table

    C. A route that adjusts automatically to network topology or traffic changes

    D. A route that adjusts involuntarily to direct frames within a network topology

9. What are exterior routing protocols used for?

    A. They transmit between nodes on a network.

    B. They deliver information within a single autonomous system.

    C. They communicate between autonomous systems.

    D. They set up a compatibility infrastructure between networks.

10. What are interior routing protocols used for?

    A. They set up a compatibility infrastructure between networks.

    B. They communicate between autonomous systems.

    C. They transmit between nodes on a network.

    D. They are used within a single autonomous system.

11. Which of the following is a global task?

    A. Addressing IP network numbers by specifying subnet values

    B. Enabling a routing protocol: RIP or IGRP

    C. Assigning network/subnet addresses and the appropriate subnet mask

    D. Setting up a routing metric to find the best path to each network

12. What metric does RIP use to determine the best path for a message to travel on?

    A. Bandwidth

    B. Hop count

    C. Varies with each message

    D. Administrative distance

13. You suspect that one of the routers that is connected to your network is sending bad routing information. What command can you use to check this?

    A. router(config)# **show ip route**

    B. router# **show ip route**

    C. router> **show ip protocol**

    D. router(config-router)# **show ip protocol**

14. Why would you display the IP routing table?

    A. To set the router update schedule

    B. To identify destination network addresses and next-hop pairs

    C. To trace where datagrams are coming from

    D. To set the parameters and filters for the router

15. If you wanted to learn which routing protocol a router was configured with, what command structure would you use?

    A. router> **show router protocol**

    B. router(config)> **show ip protocol**

    C. router(config)# **show router protocol**

    D. router# **show ip protocol**

16. In the following command, what does the last number stand for?

    `Router (config)# ip route 2.0.0.0 255.0.0.0 1.0.0.2 5`

    A. The number of hops

    B. The number of routes to the destination

    C. The administrative distance

    D. The destination's reference number in the routing table

17. An administrative distance of 15 indicates which of the following?

    A. The IP address is static.

    B. The IP address is dynamic.

    C. The routing information source is relatively trustworthy.

    D. The routing information source is relatively untrustworthy.

18. If you just added a new LAN to your internetwork and you want to manually add the network to your routing table, what command structure would you use?

    A. router (config)> **ip route 2.0.0.0 255.0.0.0 via 1.0.0.2**

    B. router (config)# **ip route 2.0.0.0 255.0.0.0 1.0.0.2**

    C. router (config)# **ip route 2.0.0.0 via 1.0.0.2**

    D. router (config)# **ip route 2.0.0.0 1.0.0.2 using 255.0.0.0**

CCNA Exam Review Questions

The following questions help you review for the CCNA exam. Answers appear in Appendix B, "CCNA 1 and 2 Exam Review Questions Answer Key."

1. If you want to add IGRP routing with autonomous system 10 to your router, which command below is correct?

   A. Singapore(config)#**router igrp 10.**

   B. Singapore(config-router)#**router igrp 10**

   C. Singapore#**router igrp 10**

   D. Singapore(config)#**router igrp 100**

2. If IGRP routing has been enabled and the last update was received 30 seconds ago, when should the next update be expected?

   A. 30 seconds

   B. 60 seconds

   C. 90 seconds

   D. 100 seconds

3. What types of routes within an autonomous system will not include subnet mask information?

   A. system routes

   B. border routes

   C. interior routes

   D. exterior routes

4. What kind of entries does a router initially refer to?

   A. Entries about networks or subnets that are directly connected

   B. Entries it has learned about from the Cisco IOS software

   C. Entries whose IP address and mask information are known

   D. Entries it has learned about from other routers

5. Which of the following best describes a static route?

   A. It is a routing table entry that is used to direct frames for which a next hop is not explicitly listed in the routing table.

   B. It is a route that is explicitly configured and entered into the routing table and takes precedence over routes that dynamic routing protocols choose.

   C. It is a route that adjusts automatically to network topology or traffic changes.

   D. It is a route that adjusts involuntarily to direct frames within a network topology.

6. What is the admistrative distance according to the output of the **show ip route** command?

   `172.16.0.0/16 [120/7] via 192.168.1.1, 00:00:22, Serial 0/1`

   A. 7

   B. 16

   C. 22.

   D. 120

7. What command will stop the IGRP routing process?

   A. Birmingham#**no router igrp**

   B. Birmingham(config)**no router igrp 55**

   C. Birmingham(config)**no router igrp**

   D. Birmingham(config)**no igrp router 55**

8. An administrative distance of 15 would indicate which of the following?

   A. The IP address is static.

   B. The IP address is dynamic.

   C. The routing information source is trustworthy.

   D. The routing information source is untrustworthy.

9. Why are routing updates not sent to a link if it is only defined by a static route?

   A. Because each node in the network already knows the route

   B. To conserve bandwidth

   C. To keep routing tables small

   D. To keep routing tables organized

10. In the following command, what does the last number stand for?

    `router (config)# ip route 2.0.0.0 255.0.0.0 1.0.0.2 5`

    A. The number of hops

    B. The number of routes to the destination

    C. The administrative distance

    D. The destination's reference number in the routing table

11. Why would you set the administrative distance really high?

    A. The network uses Enhanced IGRP.

    B. The dynamic address might be better.

    C. The network uses OSPF.

    D. The network uses only default network addresses.

12. If you just added a new LAN onto your network and you want to add the routes to the new devices to your routing table, what command structure would you use?

    A. router (config)> **ip route 2.0.0.0 255.0.0.0 1.0.0.2 5**

    B. router (config)# **ip route 2.0.0.0 255.0.0.0 1.0.0.2 5**

    C. router (config)# **ip route 2.0.0.0 1.0.0.2 5**

    D. router (config)# **ip route 2.0.0.0 255.0.0.0 1.0.0.2**

13. What command will allow you to view RIP updates as they are being sent and received?

    A. **debug ip rip**

    B. **debug rip updates**

    C. **debug ip rip updates**

    D. **show ip rip**

14. What routing protocol is being used according to the output of the **show ip route** command?

    `172.16.0.0/16 [120/7] via 192.168.1.1, 00:00:22, Serial 0/1`

    A. OSPF

    B. IGRP

    C. RIP

    D. EGP

TCP/IP Suite Error and Control Messages

Troubleshooting tools that you might use for network devices that are running Cisco IOS Software include **ping**, **trace ip route**, **telnet**, and **show arp**. The function of the IP protocol is to facilitate network communication between hosts. The design of the IP protocol allows for the addressing of hosts and networks. This distinguishes the IP protocol from nonroutable protocols that can address individual hosts but are not designed to make distinctions between networks. The acceptance of IP is so widespread that it is not just the protocol used for data delivery over the Internet; IP has also become the default internal protocol for small LANs that do not necessarily require routing capabilities.

The limitation of IP is that it is a best-effort delivery system. IP has no mechanism to ensure that the data is delivered regardless of the problems it might encounter on the network. Data might fail to reach its destination for a variety of reasons, such as hardware failure, improper configuration, or incorrect routing information. To help identify these failures, IP uses the Internet Control Message Protocol (ICMP). ICMP notifies the sender of the data that there was an error in the delivery process.

This section reviews the different types of ICMP error messages and the forms they take. Knowledge of ICMP error messages and an understanding of the potential causes of these messages are essential parts of network troubleshooting.

Concept Questions

Demonstrate your knowledge of these concepts by answering the following questions in the space that is provided.

1. What is the **ping** utility used for?

_____

_____

2. ICMP uses messages to accomplish various tasks. Fill in the following table with the list of ICMP message types.

Message	Purpose
	This tells the source host that there is a problem delivering a packet.
	The time it takes a packet to be delivered has been too long and the packet has been discarded.
	The source is sending data more quickly than it can be forwarded. This message requests that the sender slow down.
	The router that is sending this message has received a packet for which another router would have had a better route. The message tells the sender to use the better route.
	This is used by the ping command to verify connectivity.

Message	Purpose
	This is used to identify a parameter that is incorrect.
	This is used to measure round-trip time to particular hosts.
	This is used to inquire about and learn the correct subnet mask to be used.
	This is used to allow hosts to dynamically learn the IP addresses of the routers that are attached to the subnet.

3. What is Telnet used for?

_____

_____

4. What is the single most important tool used to discover layer 1 and layer 2 problems with a router? Why?

_____

_____

_____

_____

5. What is CDP used for?

_____

_____

_____

_____

6. What is an ICMP redirect?

_____

_____

_____

_____

7. What is an ICMP source-quench message?

_____

_____

_____

_____

8. What is the function of an ICMP redirect message?

_____

_____

_____

_____

9. What is the function of an ICMP address mask reply message?

_____

_____

_____

_____

10. What is the function of the ICMP timestamp request message?

_____

_____

_____

_____

11. What does a router do if it is unable to deliver a packet?

_____

_____

_____

_____

Vocabulary Exercise

Define the following terms as completely as you can. Use the online curriculum or CCNA 2 Chapter 8 from the _Cisco Networking Academy Program CCNA 1 and 2 Companion Guide_, Revised Third Edition, for help.

BOOTP

_____

_____

broadcast

_____

_____

datagram

_____

_____

DHCP

_____

_____

ICMP

_____

_____

multicast

_____

_____

Ping

_____

_____

TCP/IP

_____

_____

unicast

_____

_____

Focus Questions

1. In Figure 8-1, fill in the blanks with some of the important protocols as they relate to the OSI reference model.

Figure 8-1 Protocol Mappings to the OSI Reference Model

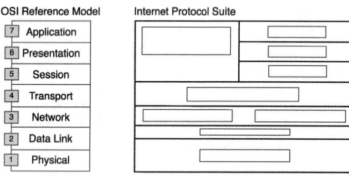

2. Figure 8-2 shows the parts of a _____ packet. Fill in the descriptions that follow based on this figure.

Figure 8-2 Packet Format

← 32 Bits →			
VERS	IHL	Type of Service	Total Length
Identification		Flags	Fragment Offset
Time-to-Live	Protocol	Header Checksum	
Source Address			
Destination Address			
Options (+ Padding)			
Data (Variable)			

_____—This is a 4-bit IP header length field that indicates the version of IP that is currently being used. The current version of IP is 4 (IPv4), but IPv6 is already being implemented experimentally and will be supported on future versions of Cisco IOS Software.

_____—This indicates the datagram header length in 32-bit words.

_____—This specifies how a particular upper-layer protocol would like the current datagram to be handled. Datagrams can be assigned various levels of importance with this field.

_____—This field maintains a counter that gradually decrements down to zero, at which point the datagram is discarded. This prevents packets from looping endlessly.

_____—This specifies the length of the entire IP packet, including data and header, in bytes.

_____—This is a 3-bit field of which the 2 low-order bits control fragmentation. One bit specifies whether the packet can be fragmented; the second bit specifies whether the packet is the last fragment in a series of fragmented packets.

_____—This protocol indicates which upper-layer protocol receives incoming packets after IP processing is complete.

_____—This field contains an integer that identifies the current datagram. This field is used to help piece together datagram fragments.

_____—This field specifies the receiving node.

_____—This field helps ensure IP header integrity.

_____- s—This field specifies the sending node.

_____—This field allows IP to support various options, such as security.

_____—This field contains upper-layer information.

3. Figure 8-3 shows a/an _____ packet. Fill in the descriptions that follow based on the figure.

Figure 8-3 Packet Format

—————————————— 32 Bits ——————————————

Source Port	Destination Port
Sequence Number	
Acknowledgement Number	

Data Offset	Reserved	Flags	Window
Checksum			Urgent Pointer

Options (+ Padding)
Data (Variable)

_____—This field contains upper-layer information.

_____- t—These fields identify the points at which upper-layer source and destination processes receive TCP services.

_____—This field contains the sequence number of the next byte of data that the sender of the packet expects to receive.

_____—This field indicates the number of 32-bit words in the TCP header.

_____—This field carries a variety of control information.

_____—This field specifies the size of the sender's receive window (that is, buffer space available for incoming data).

_____—This field indicates whether the header was damaged in transit.

_____—This field points to the first urgent data byte in the packet.

_____—This field usually specifies the number that is assigned to the first byte of data in the current message. Under certain circumstances, this field can also be used to identify an initial sequence number to be used in the upcoming transmission.

_____—This field specifies various TCP options.

_____—This field is reserved for future use.

4. A much simpler protocol than TCP, _____ is useful in situations where the reliability mechanisms of TCP are not necessary. The UDP header has only four fields: _____ Port, _____ Port, _____, and _____ Checksum.

5. In the following table, which protocols go with the listed applications?

Application	Protocols
File Transfer	
Terminal Emulation	
Electronic Mail	
Network Management	
Distributed File Services	

6. The network in Figure 8-4 is experiencing a problem: Hosts that are on a network can communicate with specific hosts on the other side of the router, but they are unable to communicate with certain other hosts. Based on this information, what is a likely cause of the problem?

Figure 8-4 Host-to-Host Communication Problems

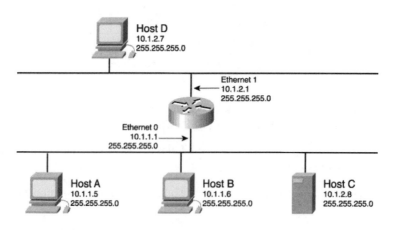

_____

_____

_____

_____

7. The network in Figure 8-5 is experiencing a problem. In some cases, you might be able to connect to hosts using some protocols or applications, but not with others. For example, you might be able to ping and host and FTP a host, but Telnet does not succeed. Based on this information, what is a likely cause of the problem?

Figure 8-5 Connection Problems with Some Applications/Protocols

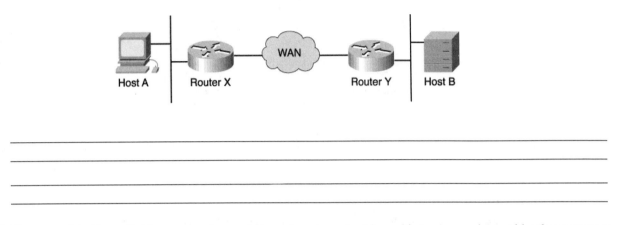

_____

_____

_____

_____

8. The network in Figure 8-6 is experiencing a problem. A router or host is unable to communicate with other routers or hosts that are known to be directly connected to the same router. What is the first thing you should check to resolve this problem?

Figure 8-6 Connectivity Problems Between Known Directly Connected Hosts/Routers

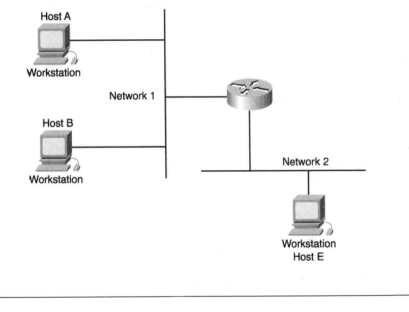

_____

_____

_____

_____

9. Fill in the problem isolation steps in the flowchart in Figure 8-7.

Figure 8-7 Problem Isolation Steps Flowchart to Fill In

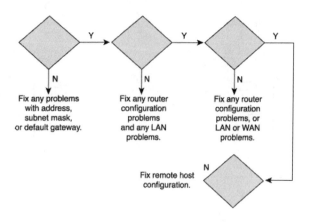

10. Based on the descriptions that follow, indicate the cause of a browsing problem.

    _____—An organization might find that domain security or some other function of a campus network requires reconfiguration on the LAN.

    _____—Name resolution on Windows hosts require proper functioning of the LMHosts and Hosts files as well as the Windows Internet Name Service (WINS) and DNS servers.

    _____—A conflict can arise when several NT systems are set up as master browsers and they send inconsistent update information that hinders convergence.

11. To check a host's routing table, type the _____ command at a command prompt.

12. List six possible causes for the following IP-to-domain name resolution problem: Local hosts can be accessed when using an IP address but not when using host names or NetBIOS names.

    _____

    _____

    _____

    _____

    _____

13. The principal reason that Internet Control Message Protocol (ICMP) was created was to report routing failures to the source. In addition, ICMP provides helpful messages such as the following:

    _____ messages to test node reachability across an internetwork

    _____ messages to stimulate more efficient routing

    _____ messages to inform sources that a datagram has exceeded its allocated time to exist within the internetwork

    _____ and _____ messages to determine the addresses of routers that are on directly attached subnetworks

    A more recent addition to ICMP provides a way for new nodes to discover the _____ that is currently used in an internetwork.

14. The ICMP Router Discovery Protocol (IRDP) uses router _____ and router _____ messages to discover addresses of routers that are on directly attached subnets.

    IRDP offers several advantages over other methods of discovering addresses of neighboring routers. Primarily, it does / does not require hosts to recognize routing protocols. It does / does not require manual configuration by an administrator. (Circle your answer.)

15. In the following table, provide a description for the listed **ping** replies.

Character	Description
!	
.	
U	
N	
P	
Q	
M	
?	

16. Two useful ping tests are an all-zeros 1500-byte ping and an all-ones 1500-byte ping. Varying the data pattern in this field (to all ones or all zeros, for example) can be useful when debugging data-sensitivity problems on CSU/DSUs or detecting cable-related problems such as crosstalk. Why?

    _____

17. A useful component of the extended **ping** command is the *Set DF bit in IP Header* option. *DF* stands for_____ _____. (Be careful of the double negative; it can be tricky on the test!)

18. The _____ command displays the contents of all current IP access lists. The output of this command is identical to the _____ command except for the fact that this command is limited to IP output only.

19. You can examine a specific access list by simply specifying the access-list _____ or _____. Fill in the correct command after the prompt in the following example:

```
Router#_____
Extended IP access list Internetfilter
        permit tcp any 171.69.0.0  0.0.255.255 eq telnet
        deny tcp any any
        deny udp any 171.69.0.0  0.0.255.255  lt  `024
        deny ip any any log
```

CCNA Exam Review Questions

The following questions help you prepare for the CCNA exam. Answers appear in Appendix B, "CCNA 1 and 2 Exam Review Questions Answer Key."

1. ICMP is an error-reporting protocol for IP.

    A. True

    B. False

2. What does ICMP stand for?

    A. Internal Control Mail Protocol

    B. Internet Control Message Portal

    C. Internal Control Message Protocol

    D. Internet Control Message Protocol

3. CMP messages are encapsulated as data in datagrams in the same way that any other data is delivered by using IP.

    A. True

    B. False

4. A default gateway must be configured if datagrams are to travel outside of the local network.

    A. True

    B. False

5. TTL stands for what?

    A. Time-to-list

    B. Time-To-Live

    C. Terminal-to-live

    D. Terminal-to-list

6. All ICMP message formats start with which of these fields?

    A. Type

    B. Code

    C. Checksum

    D. All of the above

7. Default gateways only send ICMP Redirects/Change Requests when which of the following conditions are met?

    A. The interface on which the packet comes into the router is the same interface on which the packet is routed out.

    B. The subnet/network of the source IP address is the same subnet/network of the next-hop IP address of the routed packet.

    C. The datagram is not source-routed.

    D. The route for the redirect is not another ICMP redirect or a default route.

    E. All of the above

8. What else can the Type field on an ICMP timestamp message be besides 13 timestamp request?

   A. 14 timestamp reply

   B. 14 time

   C. 14 reply

   D. 26 timestamp reply

   E. All of the above

9. Not all ICMP timestamp reply messages contain the originate, receive, and transit timestamps.

   A. True

   B. False

10. What is the ICMP type number for a router solicitation message?

   A. 9

   B. 10

   C. 17

   D. 18

11. Which one of the following is not a valid destination unreachable code value?

   A. **network unreachable**

   B. **host unreachable**

   C. **protocol unreachable**

   D. **gateway unreachable**

12. Which of the following is an example of an ICMP control message?

   A. Source squelch

   B. ARP

   C. Gateway service

   D. Echo request

13. What action will the router take when there is not enough information to forward a packet to the destination network?

   A. The router will send an ICMP destination unreachable message to the source.

   B. The router will return the packet to the source

   C. The router will notify the sender with an ICMP delay message

   D. The router will send a EIT message to the last router

14. What IOS command is used to disable ICMP redirects on a router interface?

   A. router (config)#**no ip redirects**

   B. router(config-if)#**no ip redirects**

   C. router(config)#**no icmp redirects**

   D. router(config-if)#**no icmp redirects**

Basic Router Troubleshooting

This chapter offers an introduction to network testing and emphasizes the necessity of using a structured approach to troubleshooting. It also describes the fundamentals of troubleshooting routers.

Basic testing of a network should proceed in sequence from one OSI reference model layer to another. It is best to begin with layer 1 and work to layer 7, if necessary. Beginning with layer 1, look for simple problems such as power cords that are unplugged in the wall. The most common problems that occur on IP networks result from errors in the addressing scheme. It is important to test the address configuration before continuing with further configuration steps.

Each test that is presented in this section focuses on network operations at a specific layer of the OSI model. **telnet** and **ping** are just two of the commands that allow for the testing of a network.

Concept Questions

Demonstrate your knowledge of these concepts by answering the following questions in the space that is provided.

1. Describe typical layer 1 errors.

   _____

   _____

   _____

2. Describe typical layer 2 errors.

   _____

   _____

   _____

3. Describe typical layer 3 errors.

   _____

   _____

   _____

4. Describe some network troubleshooting strategies.

   _____

   _____

   _____

5. The debug commands may disrupt normal router operations because of high processor overhead. What other problems may occur?

_____

_____

_____

_____

_____

_____

Vocabulary Exercise

Define the following terms as completely as you can. Use the online curriculum or CCNA 2 Chapter 9 from the *Cisco Networking Academy Program CCNA 1 and 2 Companion Guide*, Revised Third Edition, for help.

ICMP

_____

_____

ip default-network

_____

_____

keepalive

_____

_____

NIC

_____

_____

ping

_____

_____

Spanning Tree Protocol

_____

_____

telnet

_____

_____

traceroute

_____

_____

undebug all

_____

_____

CCNA Exam Review Questions

The following questions help you prepare for the CCNA exam. Answers appear in Appendix B, "CCNA 1 and 2 Exam Review Questions Answer Key."

1. When a technician performs basic testing of a network, which of the following is true?

    A. The technician should proceed in sequence from one OSI reference model layer to the next.

    B. The technician should proceed with any desired OSI layer.

    C. The technician should proceed with the management level.

    D. The technician should start at layer 4 of the OSI model.

2. When a technician troubleshoots a network, which of the following is true?

    A. The technician should start with a structured approach.

    B. The technician should start with an approach of his choice.

    C. The technician can start with any approach.

    D. The technician should start with client servers.

3. When a technician troubleshoots a problem on a network, he or she should do which of the following?

    A. Begin with layer 1.

    B. Begin with layer 2.

    C. Begin with layer 3.

    D. Begin with layer 4.

4. If a technician would like to test network connectivity, which basic command should he or she use?

    A. **telnet**

    B. **ping**

    C. **debug**

    D. **show**

5. When a network administrator wants to verify the application layer software between source and destination stations, which of the following commands should he or she use?

    A. **ping**

    B. **telnet**

    C. **debug**

    D. **show**

6. You suspect that one of the routers that is connected to your network is sending bad routing information. Which of the following commands can you use to verify this?

    A. router(config)# **show ip route**

    B. router# **show ip route**

    C. router> **show ip protocol**

    D. router(config-router)# **show ip protocol**

7. Why would you display the IP routing table?

    A. To set the router update schedule

    B. To identify destination network addresses and next-hop pairs

    C. To trace where datagrams are coming from

    D. To set the parameters and filters for the router

8. If you want to see RIP routing updates as they are sent and received, what command structure should you use?

    A. router# **show ip rip**

    B. router# **debug ip protocols**

    C. router# **debug ip rip**

    D. router# **show ip rip update**

9. The dynamic output of the **debug** command comes at a performance cost, which produces _____ processor overhead.

    A. high

    B. low

    C. medium

    D. maximum

10. By default, what does the router send the debug output and system messages to?

    A. The console

    B. The switch

    C. The PC

    D. The user

11. The **telnet** command provides what type of terminal?

    A. Register

    B. Virtual

    C. IOS

    D. Command

12. What does ICMP stand for?

    A. Internet Control Message Parameter

    B. Internal Control Message Protocol

    C. Internet Control Message Protocol

    D. Internet Control Message Performance

13. Most interfaces or NICs will have what type of lights that show whether there is a valid connection?

    A. Indicator

    B. Catalyst

    C. Responsive

    D. Inactive

14. Telnet is used at what layer of the OSI model?

    A. Layer 1

    B. Layer 5

    C. Layer 6

    D. Layer 7

15. Basic testing of a network should start at what layer of the OSI reference model?

    A. Layer 1

    B. Layer 2

    C. Layer 3

    D. Layer 4

16. Which of the following would not be a cause of "Serial 0 is down, line protocol is down" in the **show interface** output?

    A. A Layer 1 issue is the problem

    B. Keepalive messages are not being received

    C. The IP address is wrong

    D. There is a bent pin in the connector

17. What would cause a "Serial 0 is up, line protocol is down" in the **show interface** output?

    A. A layer 1 issue is the problem

    B. A layer 2 issue is the problem

    C. A layer 3 issue is the problem

    D. A layer 7 issue is the problem

18. Which of the following is not an advantage of a static route?

    A. Adapts to change rapidly

    B. Secure

    C. Low overhead

    D. Always predictable

19. If a route has an administrative distance of 0 in the routing table, what does this mean?

    A. The route is not available

    B. The next hop is an IP address

    C. The next hop is a connected interface

    D. The route is always available for all traffic

20. If a route has an administrative distance of 1 in the routing table, what does this mean?

    A. The route is not available

    B. The next hop is an IP address

    C. The next hop is a connected interface

    D. The route is always available for all traffic

Intermediate TCP

The Transmission Control Protocol/Internet Protocol (TCP/IP) suite of protocols was developed as part of the research that the Defense Advanced Research Projects Agency (DARPA) did. Later, TCP/IP was included with the Berkeley Software Distribution of UNIX. The Internet protocols can be used to communicate across any set of interconnected networks. They are equally well suited for both LAN and WAN communication. The IP suite includes not only layer 3 and layer 4 specifications (such as IP and TCP), but also specifications for such common applications as e-mail, remote login, terminal emulation, and file transfer.

Concept Questions

Demonstrate your knowledge of these concepts by answering the following questions in the space that is provided.

The TCP/IP protocol stack has the following components:

- Protocols to support file transfer, e-mail, remote login, and other applications

- Reliable and unreliable transports

- Connectionless datagram delivery at the network layer ICMP to provide control and message functions at the network layer

    1. The TCP/IP protocol stack maps closely to the lower layers of the OSI reference model. What function do the application protocols perform?

    _____

    _____

    _____

    2. The transport layer performs two functions. What are they?

    _____

    _____

    _____

    3. What kind of protocol is TCP?

    _____

    _____

    _____

Vocabulary Exercise

Define the following terms as completely as you can. Use the online curriculum or CCNA 2 Chapter 10 from the *Cisco Networking Academy Program CCNA 1 and 2 Companion Guide*, Revised Third Edition, for help.

acknowledgment number

_____

_____

ARP

_____

_____

checksum

_____

_____

destination port

_____

_____

flow control

_____

_____

handshake

_____

_____

HLEN

_____

_____

PAR

_____

_____

RARP

_____

_____

sequence number

_____

_____

source port

_____

_____

TCP

_____

_____

UDP

_____

_____

window

_____

_____

window size

_____

_____

Focus Questions

1. How do the TCP/IP conceptual layers relate to the OSI layers?

2. Compare and contrast TCP and UDP.

_____

_____

3. Briefly describe everything you know about the fields in a TCP segment.

_____

_____

4. Briefly describe everything you know about the fields in an IP datagram.

_____

_____

5. Briefly distinguish among IP, ICMP, ARP, and RARP.

_____

_____

6. Briefly describe how TCP uses port numbers to keep track of conversations between hosts

_____

_____

7. A SYN flooding denial of service attack occurs when a host sends a packet with a spoofed IP address. Briefly describe how a network administrator could defend against a denial of service SYN attack.

_____

_____

CCNA Exam Review Questions

The following questions help you prepare for the CCNA exam. Answers appear in Appendix B, "CCNA 1 and 2 Exam Review Questions Answer Key."

1. Which of the following best describes TCP/IP?

   A. A suite of protocols that can be used to communicate across any set of interconnected networks

   B. A suite of protocols that allow LANs to connect into WANs

   C. Protocols that allow for data transmission across a multitude of networks

   D. Protocols that allow different devices to be shared by interconnected networks

2. Which of the following best describes the purpose of TCP/IP protocol stacks?

   A. They map closely to the OSI reference model in the upper layers.

   B. They support all standard physical and data-link protocols.

   C. They transfer information in a sequence of datagrams.

   D. They reassemble datagrams into complete messages at the receiving location.

3. Which of the following best describes the function of the application layer of the TCP/IP conceptual layers?

   A. It is responsible for breaking messages into segments and then reassembling them at the destination.

   B. It acts as a protocol to manage networking applications.

   C. It exists for file transfer, e-mail, remote login, and network management.

   D. It resends anything that is not received and reassembles messages from the segments.

4. Why are TCP three-way handshake/open connections used?

   A. To ensure that lost data can be recovered if problems occur later

   B. To determine how much data the receiving station can accept at one time

   C. To provide users with more efficient use of bandwidth

   D. To change binary Ping responses into information in the upper layers

5. What does a TCP sliding window do?

   A. It makes the window larger so that more data can come through at once, which results in more efficient use of bandwidth.

   B. The window size slides to each section of the datagram to receive data, which results in more efficient use of bandwidth.

   C. It allows the window size to be negotiated dynamically during the TCP session, which results in more efficient use of bandwidth.

   D. It limits the incoming data so that each segment must be sent one by one, which is an inefficient use of bandwidth.

6. What do the TCP sequence and acknowledgment numbers do?

   A. They break datagrams into their binary coefficients, number them sequentially, and send them to their destination, where the sender acknowledges their receipt.

   B. They break down messages into datagrams that are numbered and then sent to a host according to the sequence that the source TCP sets.

   C. They provide a system for sequencing datagrams at the source and acknowledging them at the destination.

   D. They provide sequencing of segments with a forward reference acknowledgment, number datagrams before transmission, and reassemble the segments into a complete message.

7. Why does UDP use application layer protocols to provide reliability?

   A. It speeds up transmission over the network.

   B. The lack of reliability protocols makes the software less expensive and easier to configure.

   C. It lacks a protocol to sequence datagrams and negotiate window size.

   D. It does not use windowing or acknowledgements.

8. What does the abbreviation ICMP stand for?

   A. Internetwork Connection Model Protocol

   B. Internet Connection Monitor Protocol

   C. Internet Control Message Protocol

   D. Internetwork Control Mode Protocol

9. What is the purpose of ICMP messages?

   A. They put the internetwork in control mode so that protocols can be set up.

   B. They are messages that the network uses to monitor connection protocols.

   C. They are standard binary messages that act as model internetwork protocols.

   D. They are messages carried in IP datagrams that are used to send error and control messages.

10. When are TCP segments numbered?

    A. After transmission

    B. Before transmission

    C. TCP segments are not numbered

    D. TCP uses packets and not segments

11. What is the function of the three-way handshake process used by TCP?

    A. It completes research for a destination address for a datagram.

    B. It develops a cache of usable hosts

    C. It establishes a round trip connection between hosts

    D. It sends a broadcast message looking for the host TCP address.

12. How does a sender find out the destination's MAC address?

    A. It consults its routing table.

    B. It sends a message to all the addresses that are searching for the address.

    C. It sends a broadcast message to the entire LAN.

    D. It sends a broadcast message to the entire network.

13. Which of the following is used by TCP to ensure reliable delivery?

    A. Upper layer protocols

    B. Lower layer protocols

    C. Sequence numbers

    D. Port numbers

14. Which of the following best describes the purpose of checksum?

    A. It is a method for comparing IP addresses against those who are permitted access to allow entry by a host.

    B. It is a method for checking the integrity of transmitted data.

    C. It is a method for computing a sequence of octets taken through a series of arithmetic operations.

    D. It is a method for recomputing IP address values at the receiving end and comparing them for verification.

15. Which of the following best describes flow control?

    A. It is a device at the destination side that controls the flow of incoming data.

    B. It is a buffer at the source side that monitors the outflow of data.

    C. It is a technique that ensures that the source does not overwhelm the destination with data.

    D. It is a suspension of transmission until the data in the source buffers has been processed.

16. Which of the following is not a function of TCP?

    A. Path determination

    B. Synchronization

    C. Flow control

    D. Reliability

17. What is the purpose of SNMP?

    A. It monitors and controls network devices and manages configurations, statistics collection, performance, and security.

    B. It monitors the devices that are connected to one router and assigns a regular address to each host on the node network.

    C. It provides the network administrator with the ability to manage the devices on the network and control who has access to each node.

    D. It allows for the management of network security, performance, and configuration from a remote host.

18. Which of the following best describes TTL?

    A. It is a field in the datagram header that determines how long the data is valid.

    B. It is a field in an IP header that indicates how long a packet is considered valid.

    C. It is a field within an IP datagram that indicates the upper-layer protocol that is sending the datagram.

    D. It is a field in a datagram head that indicates when the next data packet will arrive.

19. Which of the following best describes UDP?

    A. It is a protocol that acknowledges flawed or intact datagrams.

    B. It is a protocol that detects errors and requests retransmissions from the source.

    C. It is a protocol that processes datagrams and requests retransmissions when necessary.

    D. It is a protocol that exchanges datagrams without acknowledgments or guaranteed delivery.

20. Which of the following best describes window size?

    A. It is the maximum size of a window that software can have and still process data rapidly.

    B. It is the number of messages that can be transmitted while awaiting an acknowledgment.

    C. It is the size of the window, in picas, that must be set ahead of time so that data can be sent.

    D. It is the size of the window opening on a monitor, which is not always equal to the monitor size.

Access Control Lists (ACLs)

Network administrators face a dilemma: They must figure out how to deny unwanted access while allowing appropriate access. Although security tools such as passwords, callback equipment, and physical security devices are helpful, they often lack the flexibility of basic traffic filtering and the specific controls that most administrators prefer. For example, a network administrator might want to allow users on the LAN to go out to the Internet through the LAN but not want the users outside the LAN to use the Internet to telnet into the LAN.

Routers provide basic traffic-filtering capabilities such as blocking Internet traffic with access control lists (ACLs). In this chapter, you learn about using standard and extended ACLs as a means to control network traffic and how ACLs are used as part of a security solution. An ACL is a sequential collection of **permit** or **deny** statements that apply to addresses or upper-layer protocols.

This chapter focuses on standard, extended, and named ACLs. In addition, this chapter includes tips, considerations, recommendations, and general guidelines for how to use ACLs and the commands and configurations that are needed to create ACLs. Finally, this chapter provides examples of standard and extended ACLs and how to apply ACLs to router interfaces.

Concept Questions

Demonstrate your knowledge of these concepts by answering the following questions in the space that is provided.

1. Each school needs two networks: one for curriculum and one for administration. Draw the LAN design for each of these networks including separate Ethernet ports on the router.

2. Devise an ACL for the router that denies users from the curriculum LAN segment assess to the administrative LAN, yet gives the administrative LAN users complete access to the curriculum LAN segment. Describe how you would proceed.

_____

_____

3. How would you accommodate e-mail traffic and maintain security?

_____

_____

4. How would you develop a firewall for the two systems?

_____

_____

5. Develop the outline for the user ID and password policy.

_____

_____

6. How would you ensure that all computers on the network have Internet access and still maintain the level of security that is required?

_____

_____

7. Outline, in detail, the security needs of this network.

_____

_____

_____

_____

_____

_____

_____

_____

8. What is the purpose of ACLs?

_____

_____

9. What condition does a standard ACL use for IP data packets?

_____

_____

10. How do extended ACLs differ from standard ACLs?

_____

_____

11. How are standard and extended ACLs differentiated in the router?

_____

_____

12. The first step to configure an ACL is to write it. What is the second step?

_____

_____\

13. Describe the significance of the wildcard mask 0.0.0.7 ?

_____

_____

Vocabulary Exercise

Define the following terms as completely as you can. Use the online curriculum or CCNA 2 Chapter 11 from the *Cisco Networking Academy Program CCNA 1 and 2 Companion Guide*, Revised Third Edition, for help.

ACL

_____

_____

address filtering

_____

_____

bit bucket

_____

_____

DDR

_____

_____

deny

_____

_____

DNS

_____

_____

extended access

_____

_____

firewall

_____

_____

IP

_____

_____

match

_____

_____

packet

_____

_____

PDU

_____

_____

permit

_____

_____

queuing

_____

_____

standard access lists

_____

_____

TCP

_____

_____

TCP/IP

_____

_____

UDP

_____

_____

wildcard bits

_____

_____

wildcard masking

_____

_____

CCNA Exam Review Questions

The following questions help you review for the CCNA exam. Answers appear in Appendix B, "CCNA Exam Review Questions Answer Key."

1. Which of the following commands would you use to find out whether ACLs are set on an interface?

 A. **show running-config**

 B. **show ip protocols**

 C. **show ip interface**

 D. **show ip network**

2. What do you call the additional 32 bits of information in the access-list statement?

 A. Wildcard bits

 B. Access bits

 C. Zero bits

 D. One bits

3. Using Router (config)# **access-list 156.1.0.0 0.0.255.255** is equivalent to saying which of the following?

 A. Deny my network only.

 B. Permit a specific host.

 C. Permit my network only.

 D. Deny a specific host.

4. When you issue a permit entry into an ACL that is accompanied by an implicit deny all, all traffic except that which is listed in the permit statement will be denied.

 A. True

 B. False

5. The **show access-lists** command is used to do which of the following?

 A. Monitor whether ACLs are set.

 B. Monitor ACL statements.

 C. Monitor ACL debugging.

 D. Monitor groupings.

6. Which wild card mask will match a host?

 A. 0.0.0.0

 B. 0.0.0.1

 C. 255.255.255.255

 D. 255.255.255.0

7. What bit in a wildcard means match?

    A. 0

    B. 1

    C. 254

    D. 255

8. What bit in a wildcard means who cares or no match?

    A. 0

    B. 1

    C. 254

    D. 255

9. If you do not supply a wildcard mask, what wildcard mask is applied automatically?

    A. 0.0.0.0

    B. 255.255.255.0

    C. 255.255.255.254

    D. 255.255.255.255

10. Which statement below does *not* describe the processing of an ACL?

    A. There is an implicit **deny all** at the end of all ACLs

    B. A packet can be permitted or denied based on the ACL

    C. Each line of an ACL is checked until a match is made.

    D. A packet that is denied by one statement may be permitted by another statement.

11. Which command below will create a standard ACL?

    A. Atlanta#**access-list 101 permit any**

    B. Atlanta#**access-list 10 permit any**

    C. Atlanta#(config)#**access-list 10 permit any**

    D. Atlanta#(config)#**access-list 101 permit any**

12. Which command below will create an extended standard ACL?

    A. Atlanta#**access-list 150 permit ip any any**

    B. Atlanta#**access-list 150 permit ip any any**

    C. Atlanta#(config)#**access-list 150 permit ip any any**

    D. Atlanta#(config)#**access-list 150 ip permit any any**

13. Which of the following is not a parameter for an ACL?

    A. Protocol suite

    B. Source address

    C. Destination address

    D. Packet size

14. A router has two Ethernet ports and two serial ports routing IP. What is the maximum number of IP ACLs that can be configured to filter packets?

    A. 4

    B. 8

    C. 12

    D. 16

15. If a match is not found in an ACL what will happen to the packet?

    A. It will be forwarded back to the source

    B. It will be forwarded

    C. It will be dropped

    D. It will be held in the output queue

16. What is the meaning of the wildcard mask 0.0.0.31?

    A. The first 26 bits will be ignored

    B. The last 31 bits must match

    C. The last 5 bits will be ignored

    D. The first 26 bits must match

17. What is the meaning of the wildcard mask 0.0.0.15?

    A. The first 27 bits will be ignored

    B. The last 31 bits must match

    C. The last 5 bits will be ignored

    D. The first 28 bits must match

18. What is the meaning of **access-list 150 deny tcp 192.168.5.0 0.0.0.3 any eq 80**?

    A. All traffic will be permitted

    B. All web traffic to the 192.168.5.0 network will be denied

    C. All web traffic from the 192.168.5.0 network will be denied

    D. Some of the web traffic from the 192.168.5.0 network will be denied

19. What will happen if the **access-list 150 deny tcp 192.168.5.0 0.0.0.3 any eq 80** is applied to an interface with no other statements?

    A. All traffic will be denied

    B. All web traffic to the 192.168.5.0 network will be denied

    C. All web traffic from the 192.168.5.0 network will be denied

    D. Some of the web traffic from the 192.168.5.0 network will be denied

Structured Cabling Case Study

For structured cabling systems to be consistent with respect to architecture and performance, they must be installed with adherence to standards. Standards are rules that define cable types, distances, and termination types. Structured cabling standards define minimum requirements for telecommunications rooms, equipment rooms, and the interconnection to the service provider. The standards call out items in such a way that many portions of the structured cabling infrastructure will be provided almost automatically. The topology is almost invariably some kind of store, with nodes closest to the network center forming the core, and nodes further away from the network center forming the access layer.

Safety is also an important part of the cabling process. Ladder safety, for example, must be observed. A fall from even a modest height can put an installer in the hospital.

Concept Questions

1. What is a Structured Cable System (SCS)? Explain.

   _____

   _____

2. Explain why safety glasses are required on cable installation job sites.

   _____

   _____

3. Explain why using the right tool for the job is important in cable installation.

   _____

   _____

4. What is the role of the UL?

   _____

   _____

5. Explain what occupational safety is and why it is important to the cabling installer.

   _____

   _____

6. What are the five subsystems of structured cabling?

   _____

   _____

7. What is the purpose of wire management?

_____

_____

Vocabulary Exercise

Define the following terms as completely as you can. Use the Appendix A from the *Cisco Networking Academy Program CCNA 1 and 2 Companion Guide*, Revised Third Edition, for help.

ANSI

_____

_____

backbone

_____

_____

BNC connector

_____

_____

bullwheel

_____

_____

cable tree

_____

_____

CENELEC

_____

_____

certification meter

_____

_____

Class C Fire

_____

_____

demarc

_____

_____

distribution rack

_____

_____

DSL

_____

_____

EMI

_____

_____

ER

_____

_____

ESD

_____

_____

F connector

_____

_____

fish tape

_____

_____

GFCI

_____

_____

HC

_____

_____

horizontal cabling

_____

_____

IC

_____

_____

IP phone

_____

_____

Kellem grip

_____

_____

MC

_____

_____

MSDS

_____

_____

multimeter

_____

_____

multipair termination tool

_____

_____

MUTOA

_____

_____

NFPA

_____

_____

patch panel

_____

_____

plenum

_____

_____

punch list

_____

_____

raceway

_____

_____

structured cabling system

_____

_____

TR

_____

_____

UL

_____

_____

vertical cabling

_____

_____

VoIP

_____

_____

work area

_____

_____

Focus Questions

1. What are the five phases that cover all aspects of a cabling project?

   _____

   _____

2. What is involved in the rough-in phase?

   _____

   _____

3. What is involved in the trim-out phase?

   _____

   _____

4. What is involved in the finish phase?

   _____

   _____

5. Why is the site survey important?

   _____

   _____

6. How does a vacuum cleaner aid in the installation of cable in conduit?

   _____

   _____

7. How is cable installed through a firewall?

   _____

   _____

8. In what application would you normally use a surface mount raceway?

   _____

   _____

9. What is covered in TIA/EIA-568-B.1?

   _____

   _____

10. What is covered in TIA/EIA-568-B.2?

    _____

    _____

11. What is covered in TIA/EIA-568-B.3?

    _____

    _____

12. What is covered in TIA/EIA-569-A?

_____

_____

13. What is covered in TIA/EIA-570-A?

_____

_____

14. What is covered in TIA/EIA-606?

_____

_____

15. What is covered in TIA/EIA-607?

_____

_____

CCNA Exam Review Questions

The following questions help you prepare for the CCNA exam. Answers appear in Appendix B, "CCNA 1 and 2 Exam Review Questions Answer Key."

1. What U.S. agency ensures that businesses comply with certain safety practices that protect workers on the job site?

   A. EIA/TIA

   B. NEC

   C. OSHA

   D. NFPA

2. Bonding and grounding is covered by which ANSI/TIA/EIA standard?

   A. ANSI/TIA/EIA 586-A

   B. ANSI/TIA/EIA 586-B.3

   C. ANSI/TIA/EIA 607

   D. ANSI/TIA/EIA 606

   E. None of the above

3. What is covered in ANSI/EIA/TIA-568-B.1?

   A. Commercial building cabling

   B. Cabling pathways and spaces

   C. Telecommunications grounding and bonding

   D. Telecommunications cabling administration

4. What standard governs pathways and spaces?

    A. ANSI/TIA/EIA-568-A

    B. ANSI/TIA/EIA-569-A

    C. ANSI/TIA/EIA-570-A

    D. ANSI/TIA/EIA-606

5. What is the TIA/EIA standard for residential cabling?

    A. ANSI/TIA/EIA-569-A

    B. ANSI/TIA/EIA-568-A

    C. ANSI/TIA/EIA-570-A

    D. ANSI/TIA/EIA-606

6. OSHA recommends

    A. Company logo stickers on hardhats

    B. OSHA logo stickers on hardhats

    C. Safety stickers on hardhats

    D. No stickers on hardhats

7. What is the most appropriate attire when working in a factory environment?

    A. Long-sleeve shirt, shorts, safety glasses, and tennis shoes

    B. Short-sleeve shirt, jeans, hard hat, and tennis shoes

    C. Short-sleeve shirt, jeans, safety glasses, and hard-sole shoes

    D. Long-sleeve shirt, shorts, hard hat, and hard-sole shoes

    E. None of the above

8. According to the NEC, select the appropriate cable types for riser installations.

    A. CMP, CMR, and OFC.

    B. CMP, CM, and OFCR.

    C. CMP, CMR, and OFNR.

    D. CMR, OFNP, and OFC.

    E. The NEC does not regulate this, TIA /EIA does.

9. What is the division between the service provider's cabling and the customer's cabling called?

    A. Backbone

    B. Demarc

    C. MC

    D. MPOE

10. What is the standard thickness of the plywood in a wiring closet?

 A. 1/4 in.

 B. 1/2 in.

 C. 3/4 in. (20mm)

 D. 1 in.

11. Into which of the following phases does cable testing fall?

 A. Rough-in

 B. Trim-out

 C. Finish

 D. Customer support

12. Computers, fax machines, and telephones are typically found in the

 A. Consolidation point

 B. TR

 C. Work area

 D. Equipment room

13. What type of cabling is between the TR and the work area?

 A. Vertical

 B. Point of presence

 C. Horizontal

 D. Work area

14. What type of topology does the TIA/EIA recommend for horizontal and backbone cabling?

 A. Ring.

 B. Star

 C. Bus.

 D. It does not matter.

 E. It depends on the type of cable being installed.

15. MSDS is an acronym for which of the following?

 A. Material security data sheet

 B. Material safety data sheet

 C. Multimeter safety data sheet

 D. Material safety determination sheet

16. Which of the following tools would be used to terminate a cable on a 110 block?

    A. Copper snip tool

    B. Wire probe

    C. Punch-down tool

    D. Diagonal cutters

17. What is the symbol for a telephone on a blueprint?

    A. D

    B. R

    C. T

    D. E

18. What color pair is terminated on pins 4 and 5 on a T568B jack?

    A. White/Blue, Blue

    B. White/Orange, Orange

    C. White/Green, Green

    D. White/Brown, Brown

19. What color pair is terminated on pins 4 and 5 on a T568A jack?

    A. White/Blue, Blue

    B. White/Orange, Orange

    C. White/Green, Green

    D. White/Brown, Brown

20. What is the purpose of a surface mount raceway?

    A. Conceal cable

    B. Protect cable

    C. Route cable

    D. All of the above

CCNA 1 and 2 Exam
Review Questions Answer Key

This appendix provides the answers to the CCNA review questions that appear at the end of each chapter and Appendix A.

CCNA 1

Chapter 1

1. B
2. C
3. A
4. B
5. C
6. D
7. B
8. D
9. D
10. C
11. A
12. A
13. A
14. D
15. D

Chapter 2

1. A
2. D
3. B
4. D
5. B
6. B
7. D
8. C
9. A
10. A
11. A
12. A
13. D
14. C
15. D
16. D

17. A

18. B

19. C

20. D

21. B

22. C

23. D

24. D

25. B

26. B

27. C

28. B

29. B

30. A

31. C

32. D

33. B

34. D

Chapter 3

1. C

2. B

3. A

4. A, B

5. D

6. C

7. A

8. B

9. A

10. B

11. D

12. B

13. C

14. D

15. C

16. A

17. D

18. C

19. D

20. B

21. D

22. C

23. B

24. D

25. A

26. C

27. D

28. B

29. D

30. C

31. C

32. B

33. A

34. D

35. C

36. A

37. B

38. C

39. D

40. D

41. B

42. B

43. C

Chapter 4

1. A

2. B

3. D

4. C

5. A

6. A

7. B

8. D

9. B

10. C

11. D

12. C

13. A

14. D

15. C

16. D

17. B

18. D

19. C

20. B

21. A

22. C

23. D

24. B

25. B

26. A

Chapter 5

1. C

2. B

Chapter 6

1. A

2. D

3. C

4. A

5. B

6. C

7. B

8. D

9. B

10. A

11. D

12. C

13. A

14. B

15. C

16. D

17. A

18. D

Chapter 8

1. D

2. A

3. A

4. C

5. D

6. C

7. B

8. C

9. D

10. C

11. A

12. A

13. B

Chapter 9

1. C

2. D

3. D

4. D

5. A

6. A

7. A

8. A

9. C

10. D

11. D

12. A

13. B

14. B

15. A, B

16. A

17. A

18. C

19. D

20. D

21. B

22. A

23. A

Chapter 10

1. C

2. B

3. A

4. B

5. C

6. A

7. B

8. D

9. A

10. A

11. B

12. D

13. B

14. C

15. B, D

16. C

17. D

18. B

19. C

20. C

21. A

22. C

Chapter 11

1. D

2. B

3. C

4. D

5. C

6. D

7. C

8. D

9. C

10. B

11. A

12. B

13. A

14. C

15. A

16. C

17. C

18. A

CCNA 2

Chapter 1

1. A

2. B

3. C

4. D

5. B

6. D

7. D

8. C

9. D

10. A

11. B

12. C

13. C

14. D

15. B

16. D

17. A

18. D

19. A

20. A

21. C

3. C

4. D

5. A

6. C

7. B

8. C

9. A

10. D

11. B

12. B

13. C

14. D

15. D

16. A

17. B

18. C

Chapter 5

1. A

2. C

3. D

4. B

5. C

6. C

7. A

8. C

9. B

10. C

11. B

12. A

13. D

14. C

15. D

16. B

17. C

18. A

19. C

20. D

21. C

22. D

23. C

24. B

Chapter 6

1. B

2. C

3. D

4. D

5. A

6. B

7. D

8. B

9. D

10. A

11. A

12. A

13. C	40. D
14. C	41. A
15. B	42. B
16. A	43. C
17. B	44. C
18. C	45. D
19. D	46. A
20. C	47. B
21. D	48. C
22. C	49. D
23. C	50. A
24. B	51. B
25. A	52. C
26. B	53. A
27. C	54. D
28. D	55. B
29. A	56. C
30. A	57. D
31. B	58. D
32. A	59. A
33. D	60. B
34. D	61. C
35. A	62. B
36. B	63. C
37. D	64. D
38. C	65. A
39. A	66. B

67. C

68. D

69. A

70. B

71. C

72. A

Chapter 7

1. A

2. B

3. A

4. C

5. B

6. D

7. B

8. C

9. B

10. C

11. B

12. B

13. A

14. C

Chapter 8

1. A

2. D

3. A

4. A

5. B

6. D

7. E

8. A

9. B

10. B

11. D

12. D

13. A

14. B

Chapter 9

1. A

2. A

3. A

4. B

5. B

6. B

7. B

8. C

9. A

10. A

11. B

12. C

13. A

14. D

15. A

16. C

17. B

18. A

19. C

20. B

Chapter 10

1. A

2. B

3. C

4. B

5. C

6. D

7. D

8. C

9. D

10. B

11. C

12. C

13. C

14. B

15. C

16. A

17. A

18. B

19. D

20. B

Chapter 11

1. C

2. A

3. C

4. A

5. B

6. A

7. A

8. B

9. A

10. D

11. C

12. C

13. D

14. B

15. C

16. C

17. D

18. D

19. A

Appendix A

1. C

2. C

3. A

4. B

5. C

6. D

7. C

8. C

9. B

10. C

11. C

12. C

13. C

14. B

15. B

16. C

17. C

18. A

19. A

20. D